Laing Art Gallery

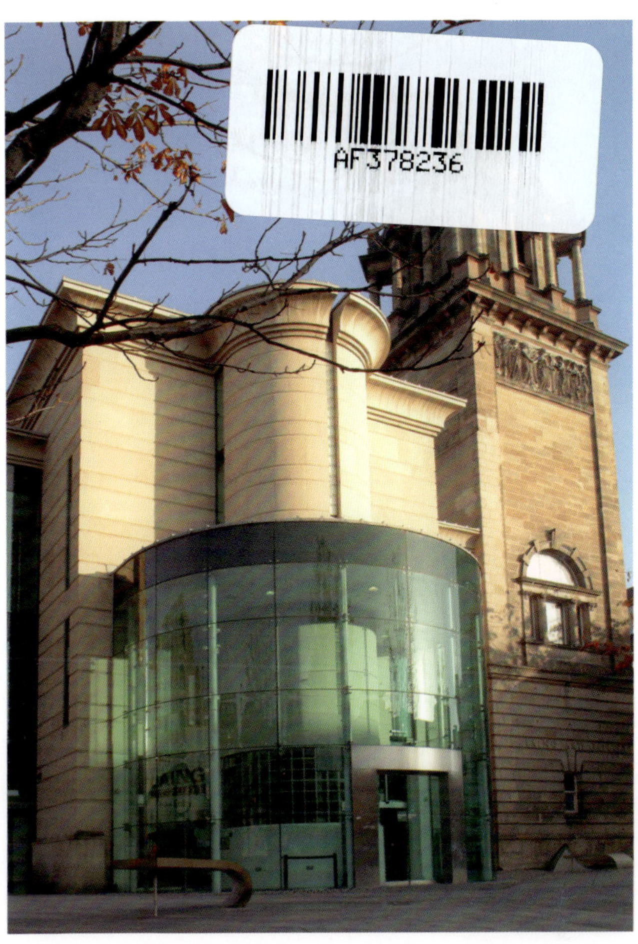

COMPANION GUIDE

SCALA

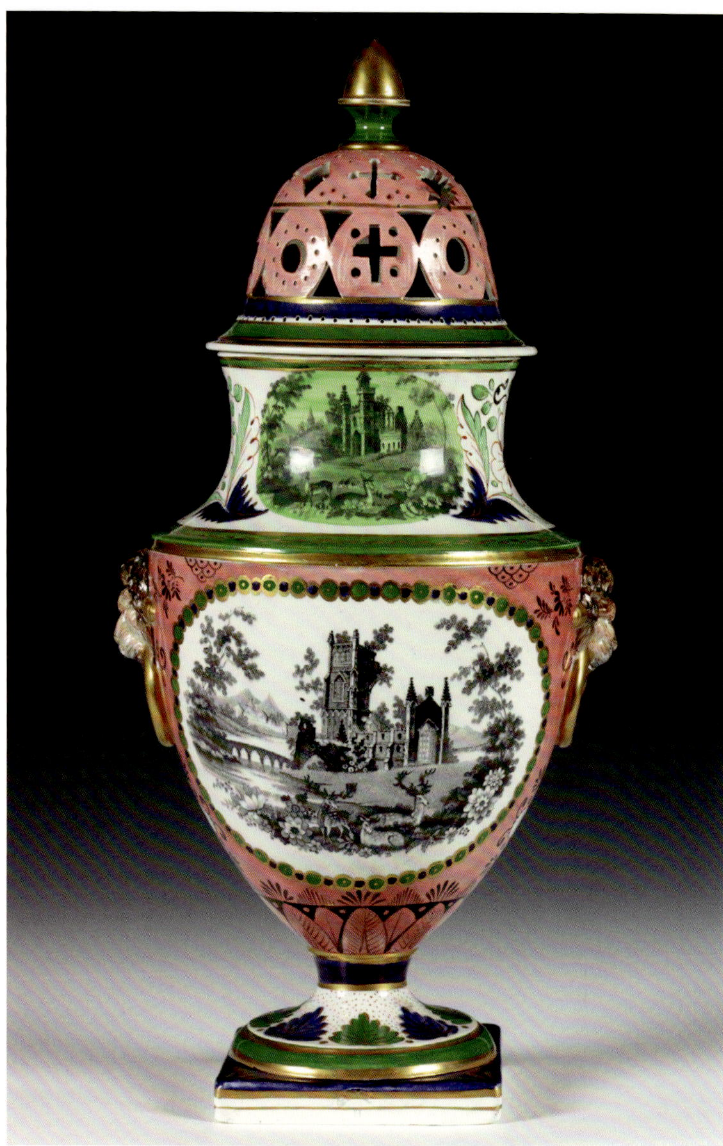

First published in 2014 by
Scala Arts and Heritage Publishers Ltd
10 Lion Yard, Tremadoc Road
London SW4 7NQ
www.scalapublishers.com

in association with

Tyne & Wear Archives & Museums
Discovery Museum
Blandford Square
Newcastle upon Tyne, NE1 4JA
www.laingartgallery.org.uk

Tyne & Wear Archives & Museums Development
Trust is a Registered Charity no. 1137867 and
a Company Limited by guarantee no. 7334262

ISBN: 978-1-85759-923-7

10 9 8 7 6 5 4 3 2 1

Project Manager and Copy Editor: Linda Schofield
Designer: Yvonne Dedman
Indexer: Diana Le Core
Printed and bound in Malaysia

Front cover:
Sir Edward Coley Burne-Jones
Laus Veneris, 1873–75
(see page 41)

Inside front cover:
The Marble Hall in the Laing Art Gallery,
early twentieth century
(see page 62)

Back cover:
Sowerby Art Glass Studio
Opalescent Glass Vase, *c*.1885
(see page 19)

Inside back cover:
Paul Noble
Paul Noble Marble Hall, 2010
Mixed media installation
Funded by the Friends of the Laing Art
Gallery and the TWAM Business Partners
© the artist

Back cover flap:
Thomas Watson (working 1793–1845)
The 'Mercutio' Racing Cup, 1824
Silver, 46 x 31.5 cm
Purchased with grant aid from The Art Fund
and Friends of the Laing Art Gallery, 1988

Title page:
**The Laing Art Gallery extension
with new entrance**, built in 1996

This page:
Thomas Fell & Company (1817–1890)
Potpourri Vase, *c*.1830
Pearlware, 43 x 21 cm
Purchased 1957

Opposite:
Detail from The Margaret and Winneford Bowl,
c.1767
(see page 18)

Foreword

Culture lies at the heart of great cities such as Newcastle. We all recognise how important it is to have a thriving business sector in a city, and I am pleased to say that this is something that is also very strong in Newcastle. However, a city without culture has no soul. Having grown up in Newcastle and spent all of my working life in the North East, I am fiercely proud of the amazing culture that this city has to offer. As Chair of Tyne & Wear Archives & Museums Joint Committee, I am delighted that, at the Laing Art Gallery, we have been able to secure significant national support for our activity programmes and to negotiate fabulous national and international loans so that the people of the North East can enjoy the finest art from across the world. The Laing manages to be both a vibrant art gallery at the heart of the city, attracting a strong family audience and many young people passionately dedicated to art, and also a wonderful place for quiet reflection where if you have a few minutes to spare you can stand in front of and admire some of the UK's most impressive art.

The Laing is an institution that is loved by people of all ages and from all backgrounds. What always pleases me, when I am away from Newcastle, is how well known the Laing is: it is truly recognised as one of the UK's special galleries. Looking at the Laing today, I can say it has never been better. We have fantastic collections, an exciting exhibition programme, wonderful staff and Friends who give a very warm welcome, and a great café and shop. If you are new to Newcastle, I hope you really enjoy your visit, and if you are a regular visitor, I hope this book gives you fresh insights into some of your favourite works of art.

Enjoy the Laing!

Ged Bell
Chair of Tyne & Wear Archives & Museums Joint Committee

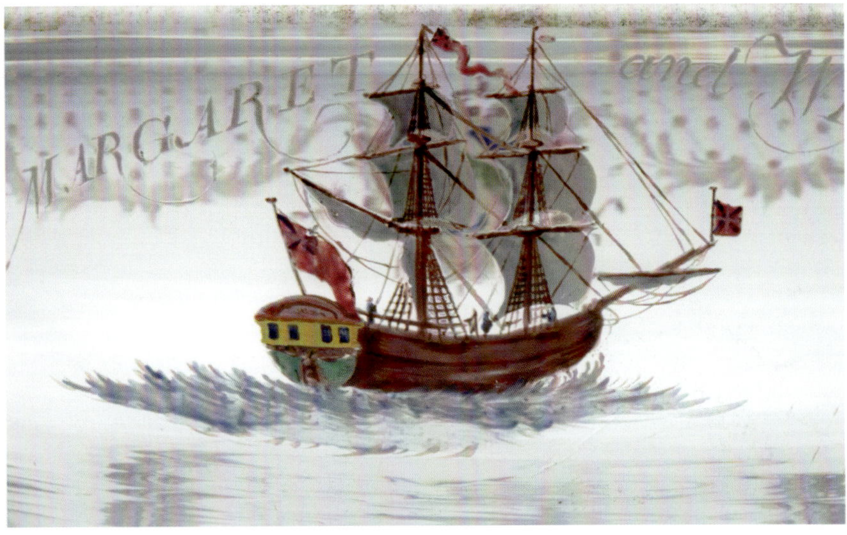

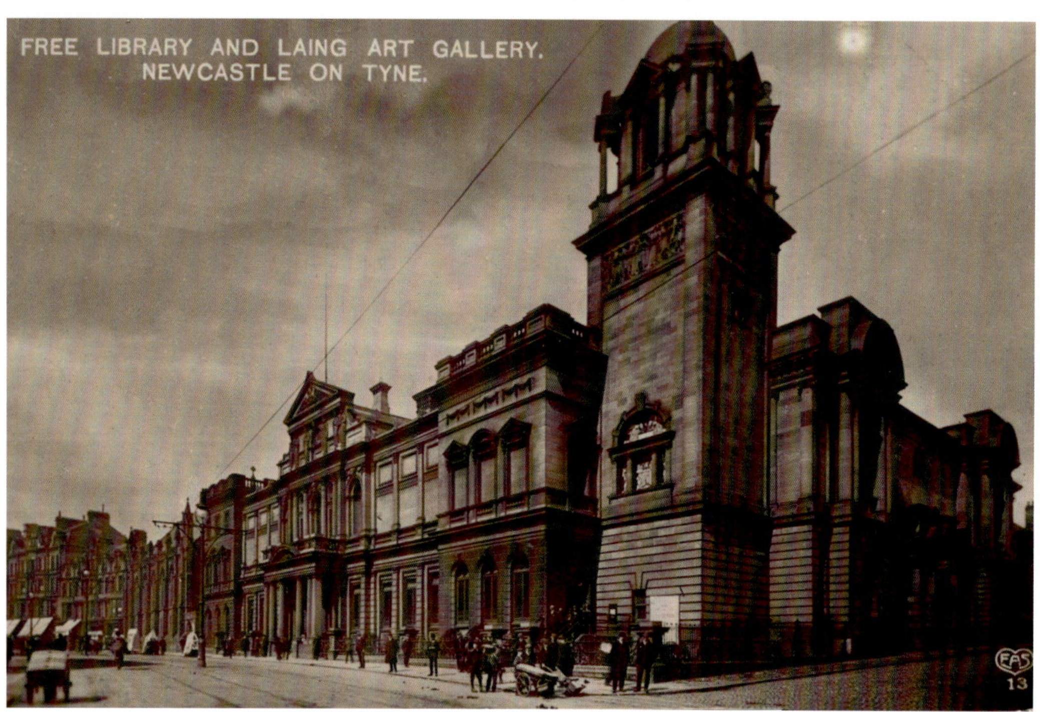

Laing Art Gallery built onto the Victorian Free Library, *c.*1920
© Newcastle City Library

The Gallery extends from the tower on the right side of the photograph. The nineteenth-century Free Library runs along New Bridge Street on the left.

Introduction

In 1900, Alexander Laing (1828–1905), a wine and spirit manufacturer, offered to build an art gallery, bearing his name, to commemorate 50 years of successful business in Newcastle. He wrote to the Newcastle Corporation, offering 'to erect and present to the city a building known as the Laing Gallery, for the free use and enjoyment of the public in perpetuity'.[1] Laing was a public-spirited businessman and gave to many charitable causes designed to improve the lives of the people of the city, including the Royal Victoria Infirmary Fund and a school for blind children. Laing's proposal was met with 'loud cheers and shouts of "hurrah!"' and was adopted unanimously.[2] Plans were prepared by a local firm of architects, Cackett & Burns Dick, and the cost estimated at £20,000, although the final cost was actually £30,000. The building, in a fashionable Baroque style with Art Nouveau detailing, was designed with an attractive and prominent tower and an ornate entrance front facing the side road of Higham Place. This site was criticised by a Councillor and the press as being too out of the way, but as no other acceptable site was available plans went ahead.

At 12 o'clock on 13 August 1901, the foundation stone for the Gallery was laid by Mrs Winifreda Adye Watson-Armstrong, the wife of Lord Armstrong the arms manufacturer, amid great ceremony and public interest. A celebratory lunch was held in the Great Assembly Rooms, Barras Bridge. Three years later, on 13 October 1904, the Laing Art Gallery was opened by Viscount Ridley, and it was so popular that police had to be brought in to control the crowds! At the opening ceremony, Alexander Laing was presented with a silver-gilt casket containing the Honorary Freedom of the City of Newcastle. A marble bust showing Laing holding plans for the Gallery was also commissioned. He died in 1905, aged 77, just two days before the first anniversary of the Gallery's opening.

There have been many changes to the building since the Gallery's foundation over 100 years ago. At the time of construction, the Gallery was built adjoining the Free Library building. When the Free Library (and associated decking) was demolished in 1968 it left a 'scar' on the southern elevation of the Gallery. Then in 1975 the original central courtyard was converted into a three-storey development, housing a staircase, further gallery facilities on the ground and first floor, and office space on the second floor. In 1996, the Gallery opened an extension with an impressive new entrance visible from Northumberland Street. The development significantly increased the Gallery's visibility from the city centre and resulted in a large jump in visitor numbers. Then, for the Gallery's centenary in 2004, a significant refurbishment was carried out, with funding from the Heritage Lottery Fund, The Barbour Trust, the Northern Rock Foundation, Newcastle City Council, and the Friends of the Laing Art Gallery (FLAG). A fine stained-glass window, designed by local artist J. Edgar Mitchell for the Gallery's opening in 1904, was conserved and reinstalled in its original location on the tower stairwell. The

Right:
James T. Cackett (1861–1928)
Laing Art Gallery, Elevation and Section, *c*.1903
Ink and watercolour on linen,
52.8 x 71.7 cm
Acquired 1983

This is one of a set of fine architectural drawings prepared by James Cackett, of local architects Cackett & Burns Dick. It shows some of the external details of the tower at the Laing Art Gallery and internal details of the Gallery spread over two floors.

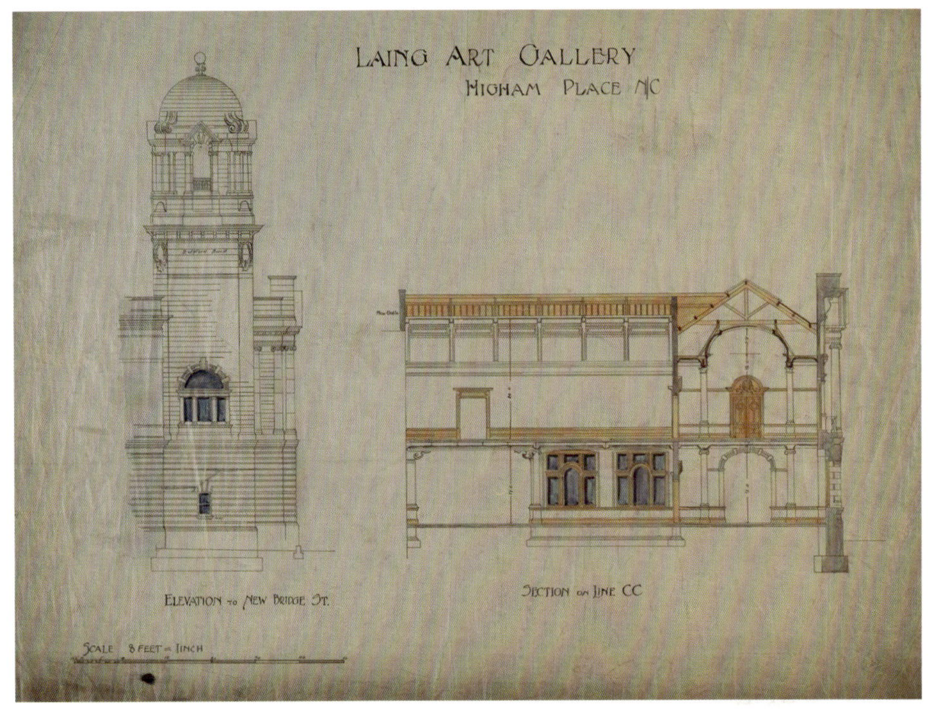

Below:
Christian Neuper (fl.1900–20)
Alexander Laing, 1905
Marble, 73.1 x 63 x 40 cm
Given by the Alexander Laing Presentation Bust Committee, 1906

When the Gallery opened, a fund was set up to commission a portrait bust of Alexander Laing. Christian Neuper, a German-born sculptor who had settled in Newcastle, created this image of Laing holding plans for his Gallery. It now stands in the ground-floor Marble Hall at the Gallery.

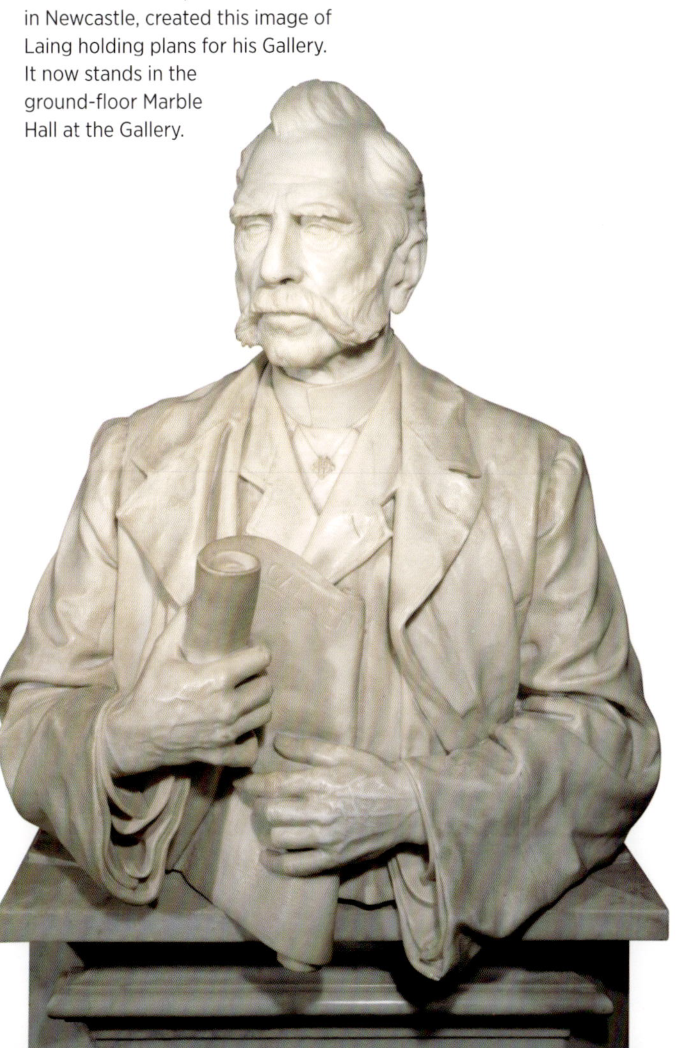

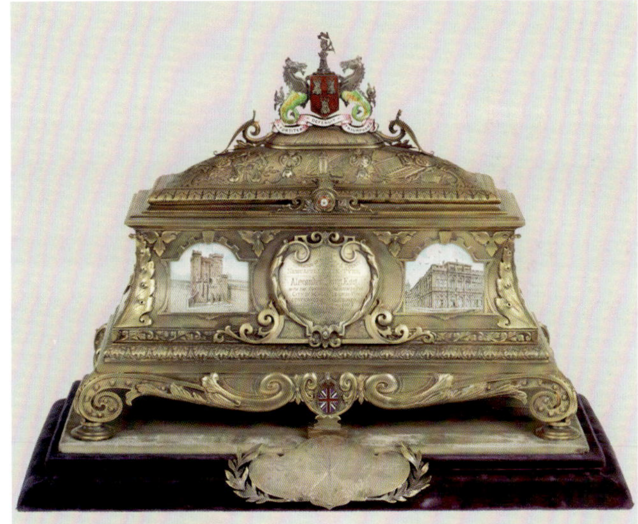

Above:
Alexander Laing's Freedom Casket, 1904
Silver and silver gilt, 31 x 43 x 26 cm
Given by Alexander Laing, 1905

At the opening of the Laing Art Gallery in 1904 Alexander Laing was presented by the Lord Mayor with the Freedom of the City, signified by this casket and the scroll it contains. The Freedom of the City carried with it many important benefits, including trading rights and exemption from tolls and charges. The casket was made in Birmingham, and the sides are enamelled with views of the High Level Bridge, Swing Bridge, Laing Art Gallery, Castle Keep and Guildhall.

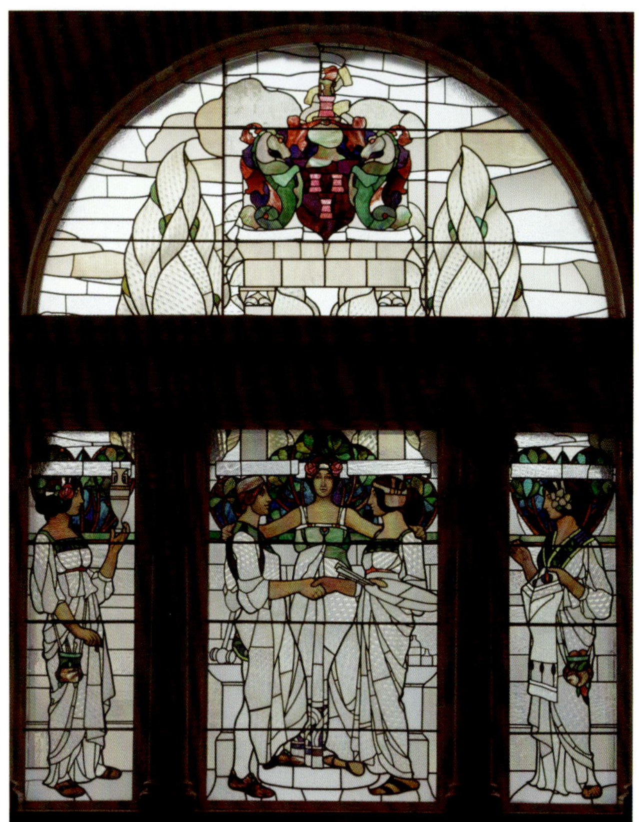

Edwardian pillared hall with its marble floor was redecorated to draw attention to the beauty of its architectural spaces, becoming a display area for some key examples of the small but significant sculpture collection. The current *Northern Spirit* gallery was opened in 2010 on the ground floor. This innovative installation showcases the creativity and excellence of art in the North East over a 300-year period. The new development has allowed the Gallery to incorporate additional artistic context and information. It replaced *Art on Tyneside*, an award-winning display of 1991, which presented stories of Tyneside art in a chronological sequence.

The Laing Art Gallery is unusual among British regional galleries in having begun as a building without a collection. Alexander Laing was not a connoisseur or collector, and when he wrote to the Newcastle Corporation in 1900 offering to provide the building, he stated that he was confident 'that by the liberality of the inhabitants it would soon be supplied with pictures and statuary for the encouragement and development of British Art'.[3] The first curator, C. Bernard Stevenson, was known to joke that he might need to resort to exhibiting the wood shavings left by joiners for the opening exhibition in 1904. The *Special Inaugural Exhibition by British and Foreign Artists* was a triumph and concentrated on works by the British School from William Hogarth onwards, supplied by loans from local collectors and national institutions. Because of its success the Council decided to build up a permanent collection along

J. Edgar Mitchell (1871–1921)
The Marriage of the Arts, *c*.1904
Stained glass, *c*.400 x 360 cm

J. Edgar Mitchell designed the glazing for many buildings in the area, including this Arts and Crafts-style stair window for the Gallery's opening in 1904. The image is highly symbolic, with figures representing different types of art brought together in one place, which was the purpose of the Laing Art Gallery itself. The window frame is designed to look like a Classical temple and the crest of the City of Newcastle appears in the top section.

Right:
The *Special Inaugural Exhibition by British and Foreign Artists*, 1904

A view of the first-floor gallery D at the *Special Inaugural Exhibition*. On the walls are paintings on loan from Oldham Art Gallery, Dundee Art Galleries and Museums, and The Lady Lever Art Gallery, Port Sunlight Village. Above the door hangs George Boughton's *A Diana of the Pastures* (*c*.1901), loaned to the exhibition by the artist.

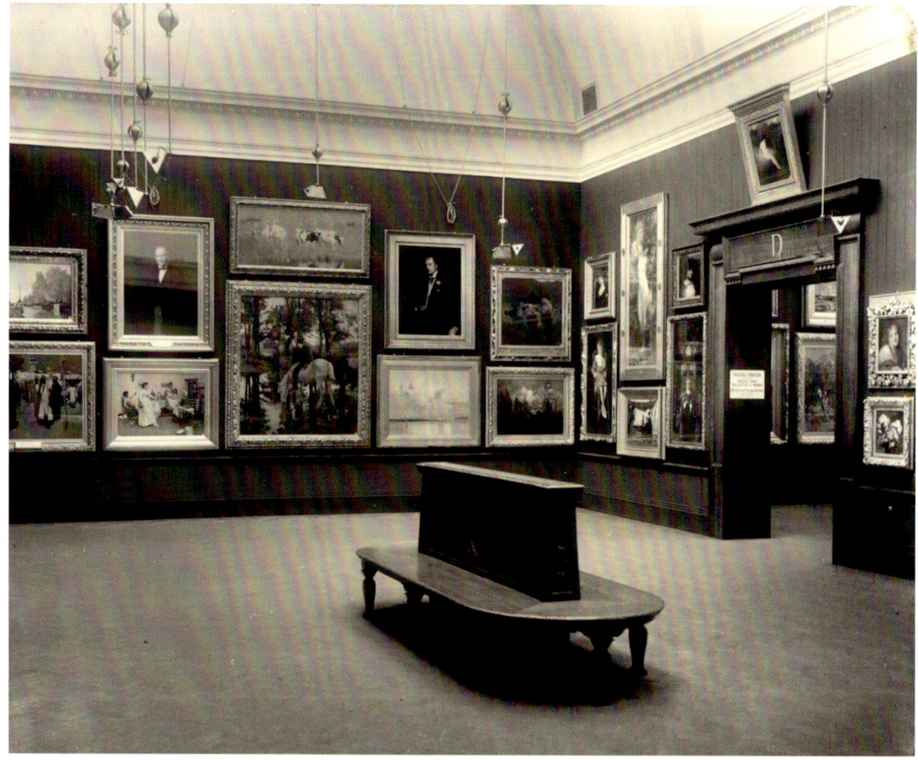

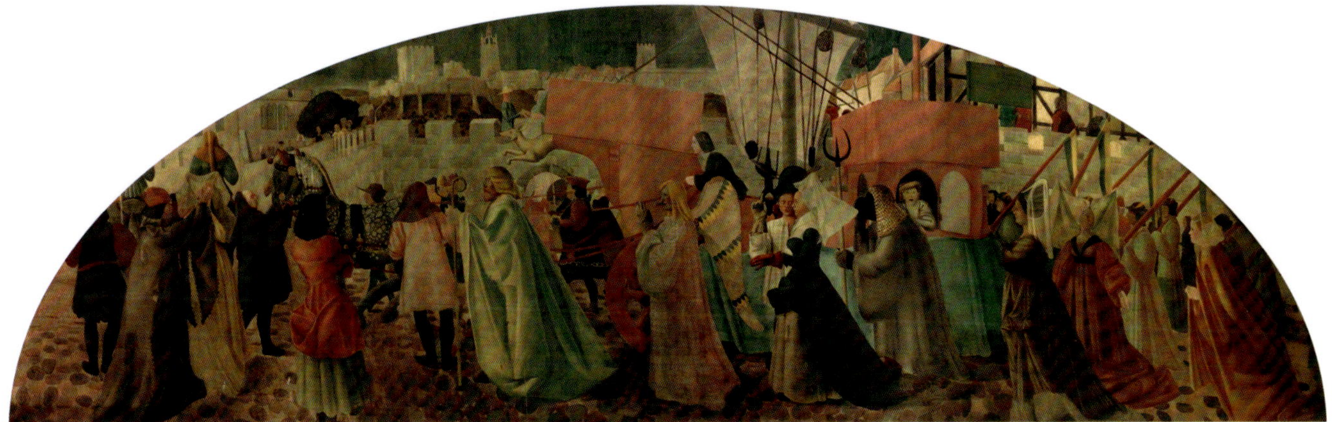

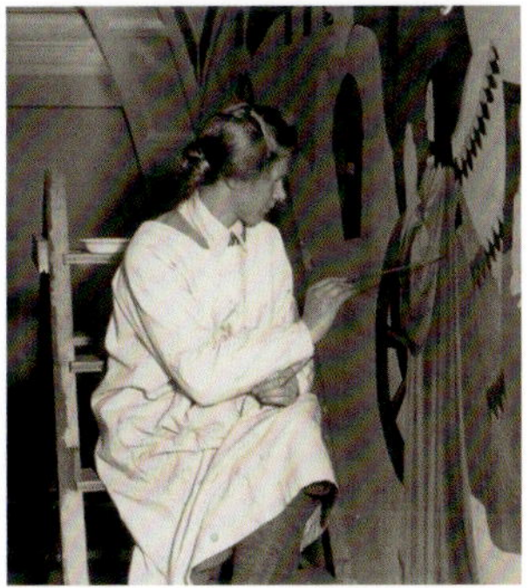

Right:

Louisa Hodgson painting the lunette in gallery C, *Corpus Christi Day in Newcastle upon Tyne c.1450 (The Shipwright's Guild)*, *c.*1933

Louisa Hodgson sitting on a ladder working on 'Corpus Christi Day'. The lunettes were painted in situ, but not directly onto the walls. Each painting is on a shaped and stretched canvas set into the top of the wall.

Above:

Louisa Hodgson (1905–1980)

Corpus Christi Day in Newcastle upon Tyne c.1450 (The Shipwright's Guild), 1934

Tempera on canvas, 245 x 851.5 cm
Purchased with grant aid from the William Glover Fund, 1934

One of eight scenes of Newcastle's history by different artists, commissioned by the Gallery between about 1924 and 1934, this painting shows the Shipwrights, who were important members of Newcastle's Craft Guild. They are on their way to perform their annual guild play *Noah's Ark*, in about 1450. Behind them are the city walls, with the castle and the churches of St Nicholas and All Hallows.

similar lines and this decision set the tone for the British character of the Laing's fine art collections.

Alexander Laing's confidence that local people would donate to the Gallery proved correct, and from its earliest days the Laing benefited from a large number of important gifts and bequests, many of them from prominent industrialists and other public figures. One of the earliest gifts of groups of artworks came from John Lamb in 1909, followed by donations from William Glover in 1920, and George E. Henderson in 1934 and 1937. Much of the collection has, however, been acquired by purchase. National funding has been obtained successfully for many key purchases, particularly from the National Art Collections Fund, the Victoria and Albert Museum Purchase Grant Fund, and in more recent years the Heritage Lottery Fund. Locally, the Friends of the Laing Art Gallery's support is instrumental in building the collection.

The collection of nineteenth-century British oil paintings is significant, with two world-famous masterpieces of Pre-Raphaelite art: William Holman Hunt's *Isabella and the Pot of Basil* is universally recognised as among his most important compositions; and Edward Burne-Jones's *Laus Veneris* is regarded by many authorities as the artist's single finest and most representative work. The North East was home to a small but dedicated group of collectors of Pre-Raphaelite art, and

some of their more noteworthy pieces have made their way into the Gallery's collection. The local collector James Leathart, a lead manufacturer, commissioned a family portrait from Arthur Hughes, *Mrs Leathart and Her Three Children*, which was purchased for the collection in 1998.

Outstanding works by Sir Lawrence Alma-Tadema, John William Waterhouse and Sir Edward Poynter demonstrate the revival in Classical interest during the later nineteenth century. There are examples of all the major genres within Victorian art, including work by John Frederick Lewis and Alfred de Bréanski, while Sir Edwin Landseer, court painter to Queen Victoria, is represented by several paintings, including a magnificent pair of animal portraits commissioned by the Earl of Tankerville in 1867 for the Great Hall of Chillingham Castle. A particular strength of the collection lies in the representation of the Rustic Naturalists: Sir George Clausen, Henry Herbert La Thangue and their contemporaries. Clausen's *Stone Pickers* was acquired early in the history of the Laing's collection, being purchased in 1907 from an annual exhibition, *Artists of the Northern Counties*, which was an opportunity for up-and-coming artists based in the North to show and sell their work.

The Gallery has the most comprehensive collection in the world of the work of locally born British Romantic artist John Martin. Two outstanding examples of his work include *The*

Destruction of Sodom and Gomorrah and *The Bard.* His powerful and unique vision is now represented in collections around the world, including Tate Britain. From the eighteenth century, the collection contains a particularly fine group of portraits, ranging from large-scale works by Thomas Hudson and Allan Ramsay, and one of Sir Joshua Reynolds's most highly regarded full-length portraits, *Mrs Riddell* (1763), which was purchased in 1965. There are also fascinating conversation and genre pieces by Francis Hayman and Johann Zoffany. The rapidly changing styles of the later eighteenth century are demonstrated by Sir Henry Raeburn and James Ward, among others.

The important collection of early twentieth-century paintings ranges from Edwardian portraits by John Singer Sargent and Augustus John, to an unusual self-portrait by Sir William Orpen, and *Holy Motherhood*, a Symbolist-influenced piece by Thomas Cooper Gotch. The work of the Newlyn School of artists is demonstrated most notably within the collection by Laura and Harold Knight and Ernest and Dod Proctor. The Camden Town Group is represented by Sir Walter Sickert and Malcolm Drummond, the Bloomsbury Group by Duncan Grant, and the Glasgow Boys by Ernest Atkinson Hornel. Pre- and post-war abstraction is less well represented, but there are major works by Victor Pasmore, who taught for a time at Newcastle University, William Gear, Terry Frost and Ben Nicholson. A number of major contemporary works have also been added to the collection over the last ten years. These include paintings by Ron B. Kitaj and John Bratby, together with large-scale works by Steven Campbell, Adrian Wiszniewski and Gillian Ayres.

Although the collection is predominantly British, there is a small group of European paintings, including the Flemish painter Thierri Bouts's fifteenth-century work *The Miracle of the Gallows*, Gregorio de Ferrari's Italian Baroque *Flight into Egypt*, and an exquisite sixteenth-century north European devotional image, *The Adoration of the Magi.* Paul Gauguin's *The Breton Shepherdess* is another of the great masterpieces in the collection. Given by the National Art Collections Fund in 1945, it was selected for the Laing from a bequest of French and English Impressionist and Post-Impressionist works, drawn from the collection of Mrs D.M. Fulford.

There is an important historical watercolour collection, which includes pictures by J.M.W. Turner, Thomas Girtin, David Cox, Samuel Palmer, Myles Birket Foster, Eric Ravilious and Elizabeth Blackadder. Central to this is a collection of watercolours given in 1942 by the Walker Mechanics Institute, which had bought the pictures as part of its programme to improve the education

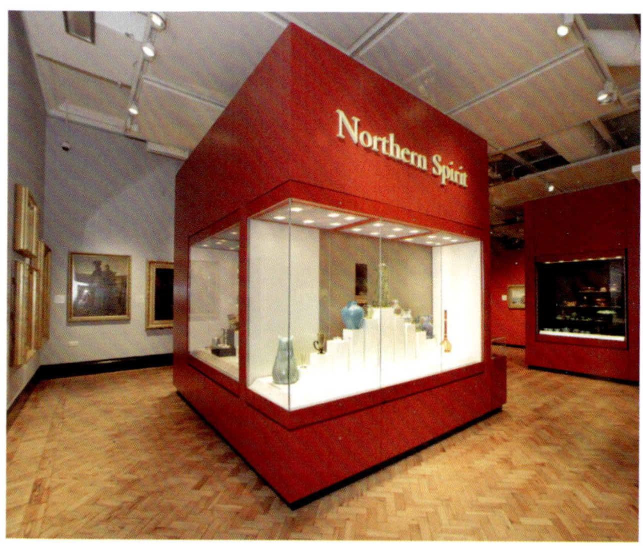

Northern Spirit: 300 years of art in the North East (opened 2010)

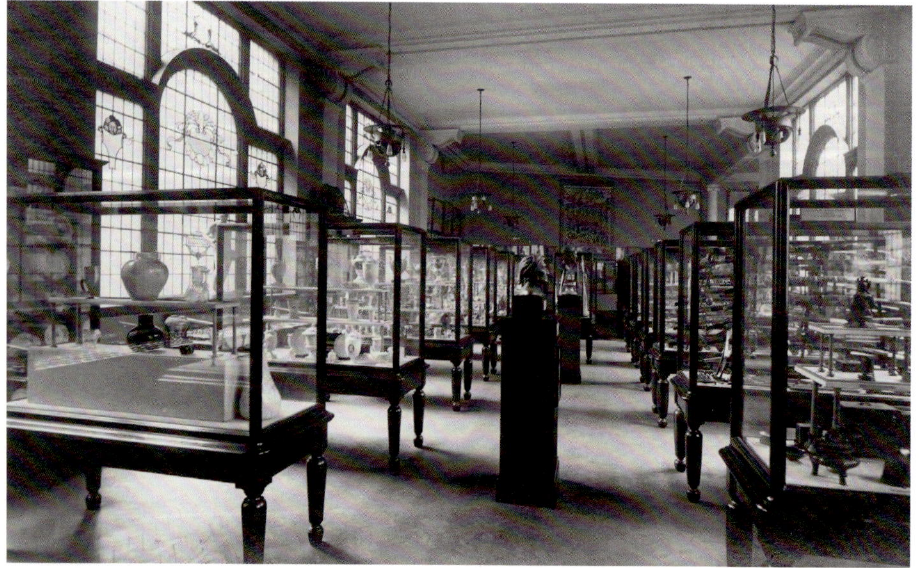

The ground-floor gallery (now *Northern Spirit*), *c.*1930–50

The ground-floor gallery used to be known as 'the back museum'. Its displays followed the model of the Victoria and Albert Museum in London. They focused on the decorative arts collection, and included ceramics, silverware, pewter and coins, as well as archaeology. This display was redeveloped during the 1990s to create the *Art on Tyneside* gallery, which was replaced by *Northern Spirit* in 2010.

Arthur Hughes (1832–1915)
Portrait of Mrs Leathart and Her Three Children, 1863–65
Oil on canvas, 54.7 x 92.7 cm
Purchased with grant aid from the Victoria and Albert Museum Purchase Grant Fund, Heritage Lottery Fund, The Art Fund, Friends of the Laing Art Gallery and Trustees of the John Wigham Richardson Bequest, 1998

The Newcastle industrialist and art collector James Leathart commissioned this picture of his young family from Arthur Hughes, who was one of the younger generation of Pre-Raphaelite artists. He painted the heads at the family's Gateshead home and finished the picture in his London studio.

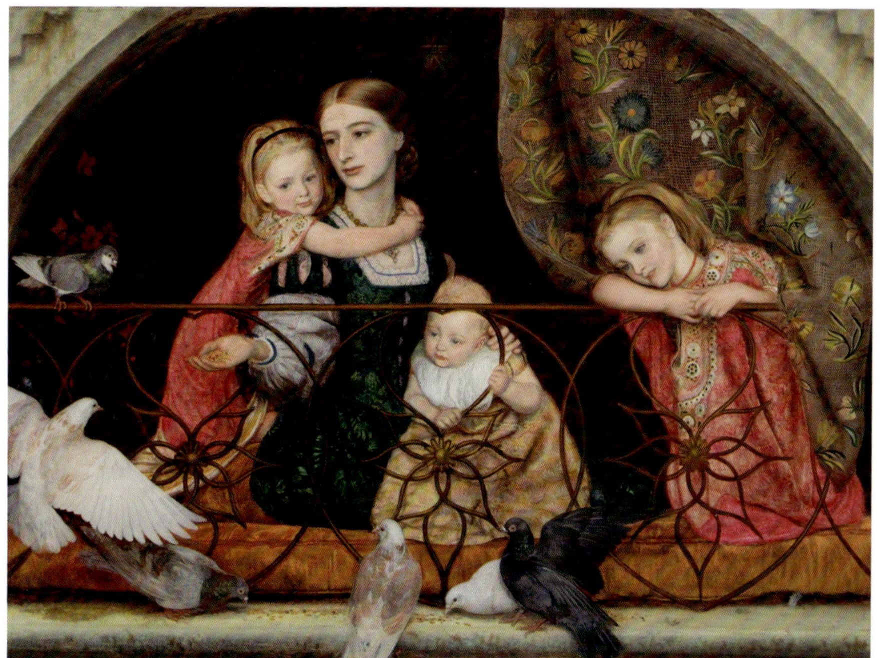

and skills of its members, who were mostly shipyard workers. Contemporary acquisitions have included watercolours by Laura Lancaster and Marlene Dumas. The small sculpture collection features some outstanding works by artists including Henry Moore, Jacob Epstein and George Frederick Watts.
. The extensive print collection features work by the exceptional local wood-engraver Thomas Bewick, together with related material such as woodblocks, preparatory studies, engraving tools and books. Local topographical and portrait prints are very well represented, together with fine mezzotints after John Martin, and examples of work from leading artists from the eighteenth to the twentieth centuries, including J.M. Whistler, Walter Sickert and Thomas Rowlandson. There is a good collection of contemporary artists' prints with works by Paula Rego, Allen Jones, Richard Hamilton, Eduardo Paolozzi, Elizabeth Frink and David Hockney.

The decorative arts collections are varied and extensive, with a particular emphasis on works made in the North East, and feature glass, ceramics, silver and metalwork. There is cut and engraved glass produced at many of the region's glass-houses in the early nineteenth century; Dutch engraved glass from the eighteenth century, including a signed piece by Jacob Sang; and outstanding eighteenth-century Beilby enamelled glass. The world importance of the North East in the production of pressed glass from the mid-nineteenth century is also represented by a wide-ranging collection of objects and archival material from the leading manufacturers. A comprehensive collection of Tyneside pottery is complemented by examples from major British and European makers – including Wedgwood, Derby, Meissen and Sevres – while the silver collection features significant examples of rare Newcastle silver, such as the work of the Newcastle Handicraft Company, an influential regional Arts and Crafts Guild. A notable collection of Japanese prints and objects, including ivories and bronzes, was donated by Albert H. Higginbottom in 1919.

Changing displays and exhibitions go on show to highlight varied aspects of the art collections, complementing the long-running displays in *Northern Spirit* on the ground floor and the *18th and 19th-Century Paintings* gallery on the first floor. The exhibition programme is wide-ranging, featuring historical and contemporary art, both separately and in combination, and also includes occasional commissions. It is a tribute to the knowledge and foresight of successive curators that the Laing has amassed what is now a Designated collection, recognised as being of national significance. Over the past 100 years, the Laing has been transformed from an empty building to the North East's premier art gallery.

Julie Milne   Chief Curator of Art Galleries

Notes
1. Letter from Alexander Laing to Newcastle Council, 17 January 1900, read at the meeting held on 7 February 1900, quoted in Council Minutes, signed, 10 January 1900 – 19 March 1902, p.33.
2. Quoted in *The Laing Art Gallery 1904–1979*, Tyne & Wear County Council Museums, 1979, p.1.
3. Letter from Alexander Laing to Newcastle Council, op. cit., p.33.

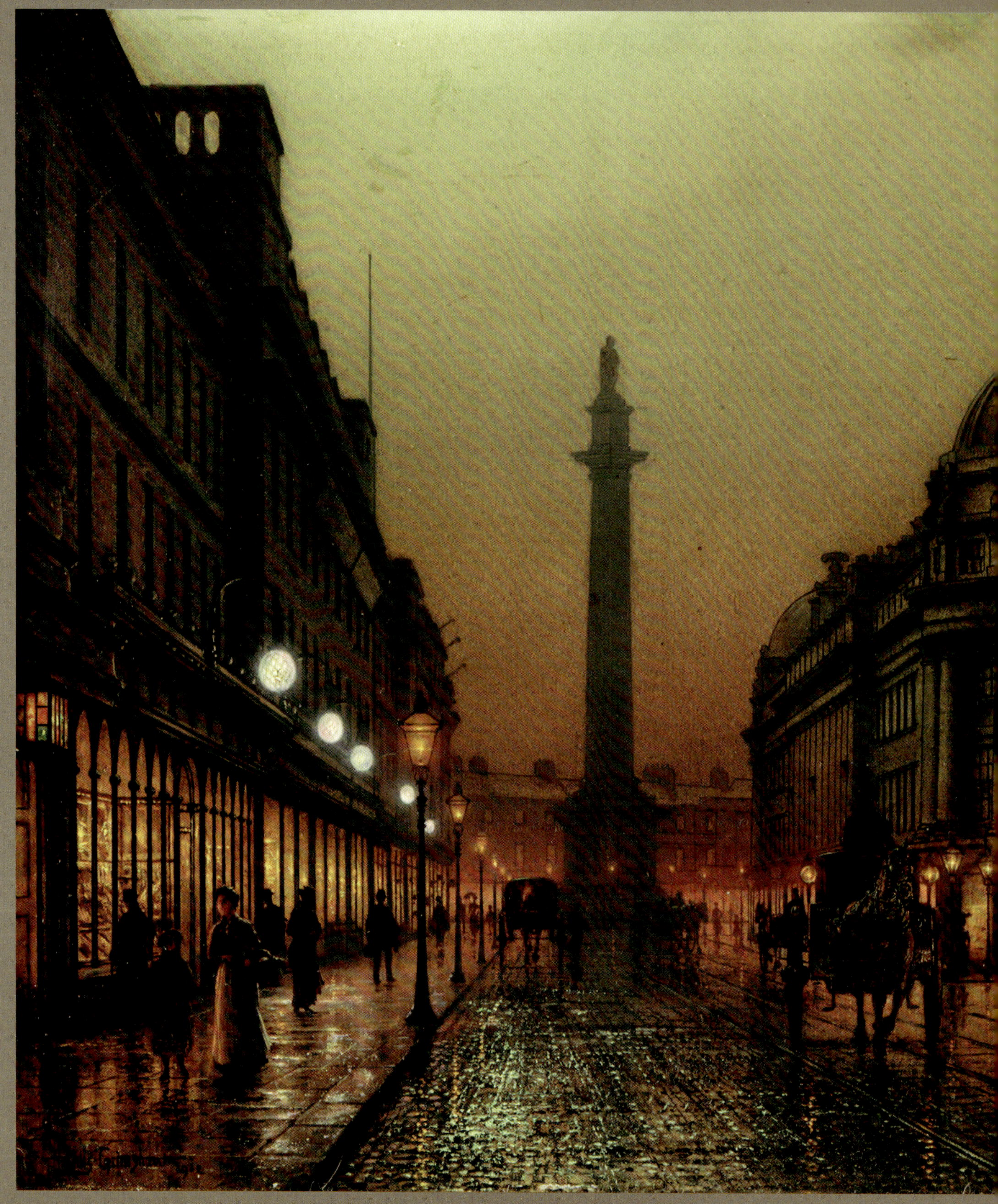

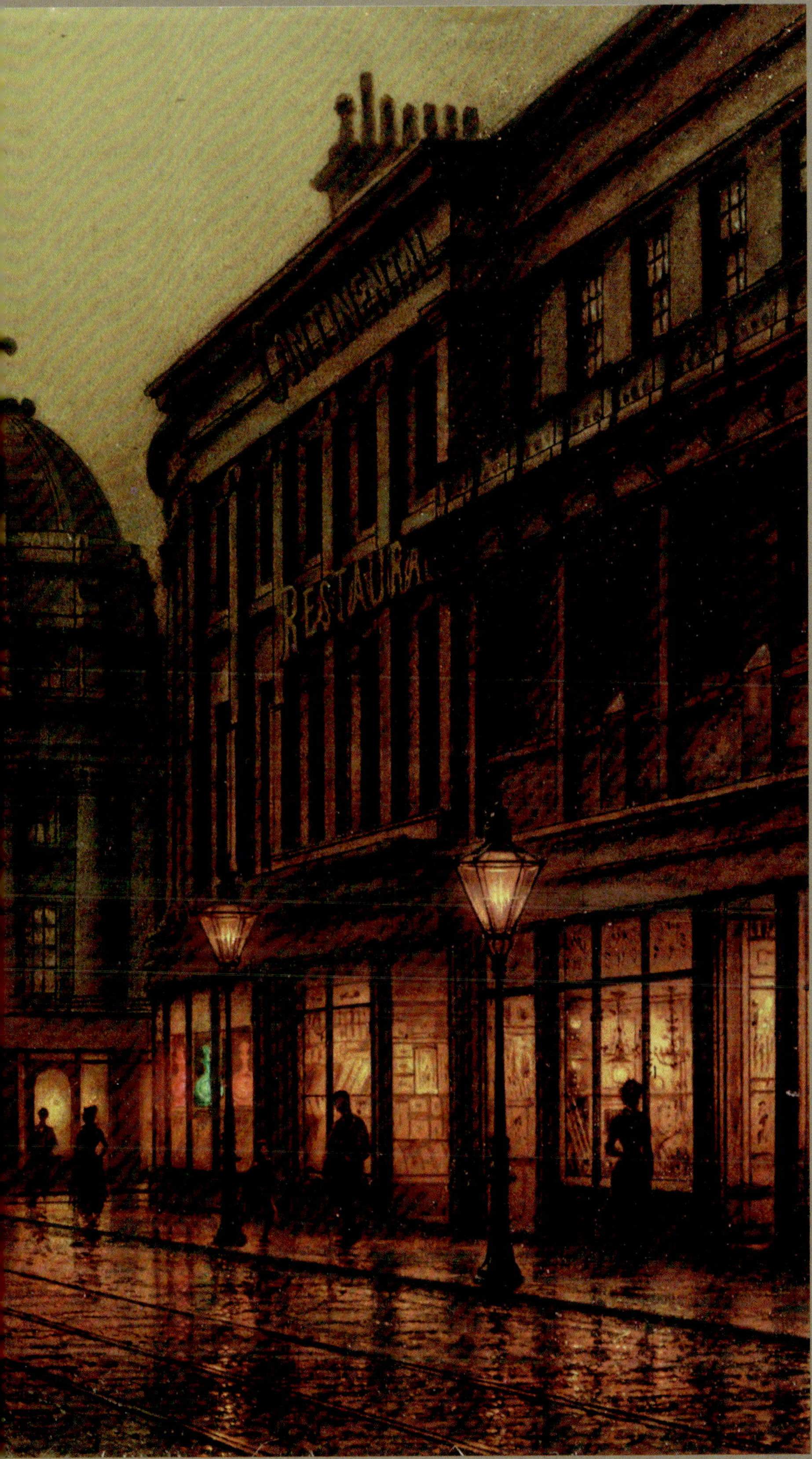

Selected Works from the Collections

Text by
Marie-Thérèse Mayne
Lesley Richardson
Sarah Richardson

Louis H. Grimshaw (1870–1943)
Grainger Street, Newcastle upon Tyne,
1902
Oil on board, 41.5 x 56.7 cm
Purchased 1978

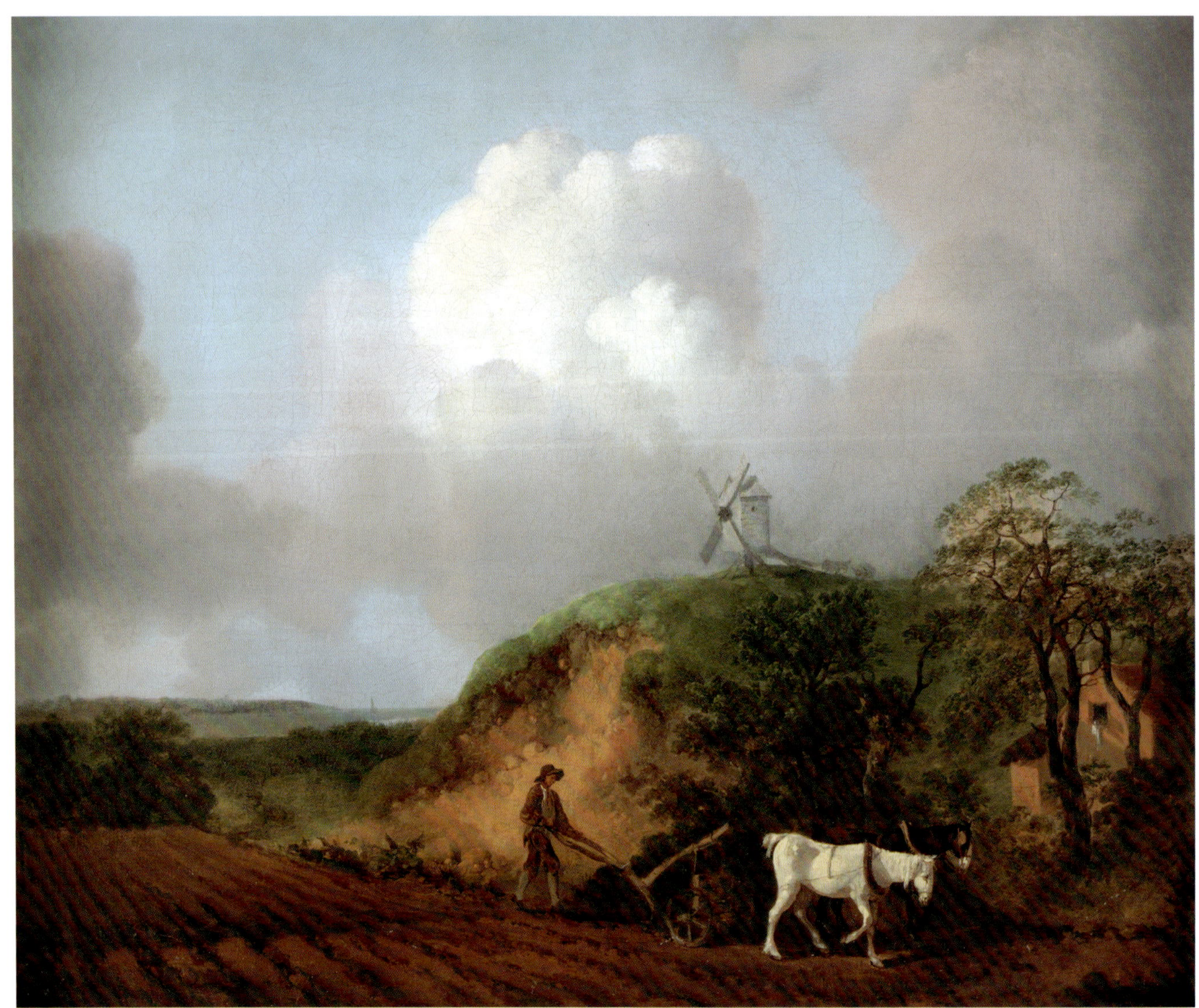

Thomas Gainsborough (1727–1788)
Peasant Ploughing with Two Horses, 1750–53
Oil on canvas, 49.1 x 59.1 cm
Purchased with grant aid from the Victoria and Albert Museum Purchase Grant Fund, Heritage Lottery Fund, Friends of the Laing Art Gallery and John Wigham Richardson Bequest, 2003

Although known as one of the leading portrait painters of the late eighteenth century, Gainsborough much preferred painting landscape and rustic scenes, and in his private letters he often recorded his impatience with clients who constantly demanded portraits. Gainsborough's art was key to the development of naturalistic landscape painting in Britain in the second half of the eighteenth century and provided the basis for naturalistic and romantic landscape art of the nineteenth century.

Peasant Ploughing with Two Horses is a significant landscape from the period he was working in Ipswich (*c*.1752–59), when he developed an original landscape style fusing the naturalism of Dutch painting with the lighter elements of French rococo art. The soft treatment of the clouds, the loose handling of the sandy bank and the generalised description of the terrain point to the influence of the Dutch seventeenth-century artist Jan Wijnants. Like other paintings from Gainsborough's Ipswich period, the colouring is warmer than in his earlier pictures and illustrates his sensitive handling of light and atmospheric recession. The subject matter reflects eighteenth-century sentiment regarding the importance of simple rural life, and this is the first instance of Gainsborough including a plough-man, which became one of his favourite motifs.

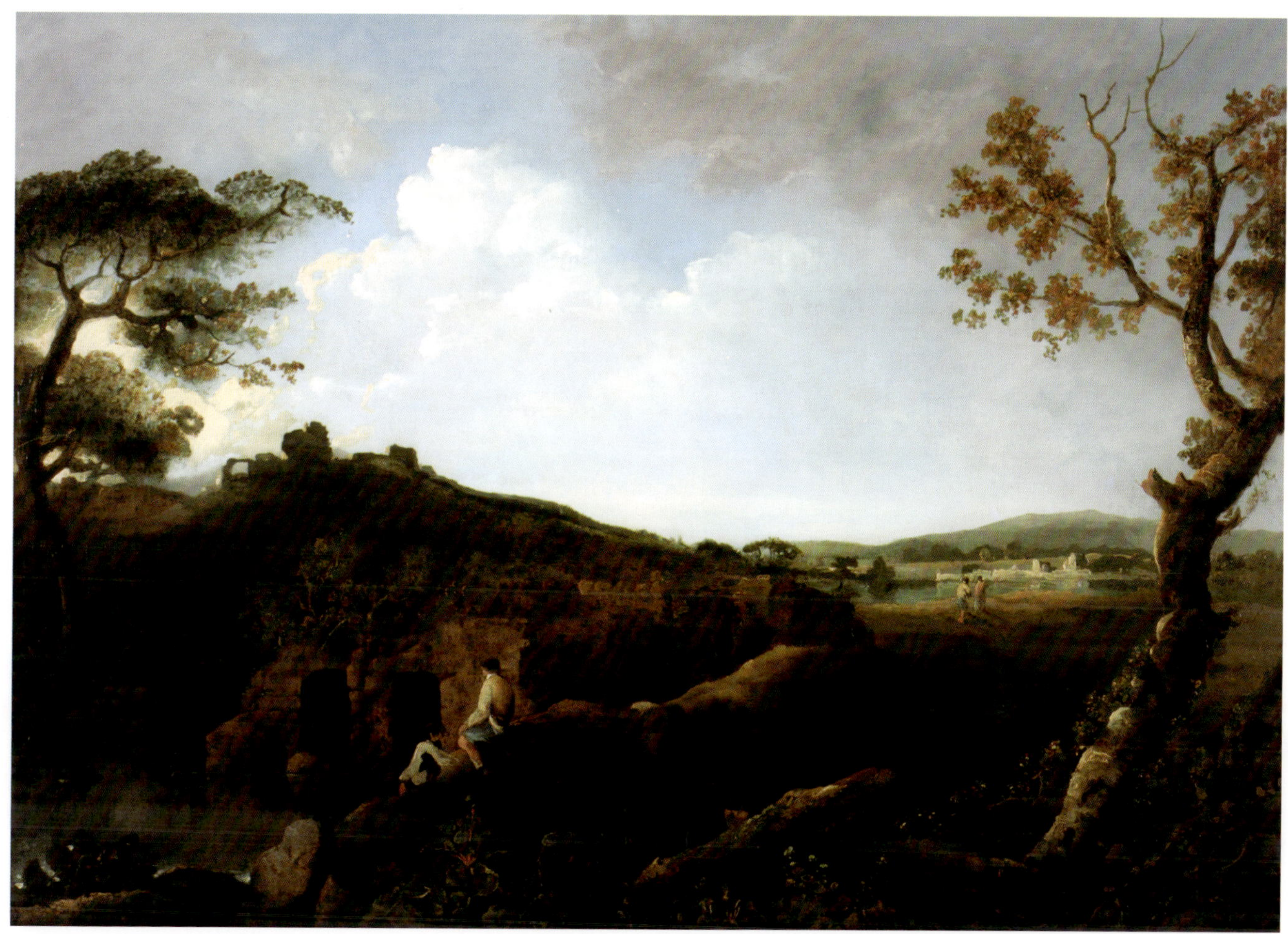

Richard Wilson (1714–1782)
The Alban Hills, c.1751–57
Oil on canvas, 73.6 x 101.4 cm
Purchased 1954

During the eighteenth century British artists began to paint landscapes for their own sake, rather than just as records of gentlemen's estates or as backgrounds to figure subjects. A founding member in 1768 of the Royal Academy of Arts, London, the Welsh artist Richard Wilson was one of the first to explore this method of working, and was also interested in capturing the atmospheric effects of weather in his landscape scenes.

Wilson's Italian-style landscapes were very popular with collectors. He spent several years in Italy, living in Rome from 1752 to 1757. *The Alban Hills* was begun in Italy, but it is likely that it was finished only after the artist returned to England. This poetic view of scenery and Roman ruins near Lake Albano was inspired by the great seventeenth-century landscape painters Claude Lorrain and Gaspard Dughet, and also by Wilson's own experience of the Roman Campagna, the low-lying area around the city of Rome renowned for its pastoral beauty. An essential part of the Grand Tour, the Campagna was favoured by British artists and tourists, who made short excursions from Rome to see its classical ruins, Renaissance villas, gardens, lakes and hills. During the eighteenth and nineteenth centuries, it was one of the most painted landscapes in Europe.

Thomas Bewick (1753–1828)

Thomas Bewick was born at Cherryburn House, a small farm near Mickley in Northumberland. The eldest of eight children, he showed an interest and talent for drawing from an early age. When he was 14 he was apprenticed to Newcastle engraver Ralph Beilby, who owned a successful workshop in Newcastle. The Beilby family was especially renowned for enamel painting on glass, but Ralph specialised in engraving on wood and metal. Bewick was apprenticed for seven years and soon showed a talent for woodcut engraving. On completing his apprenticeship he travelled for a while, then returned to Newcastle in 1777 and entered into a business partnership with Beilby.

Soon afterwards Bewick began the first of his works in natural history, *A General History of Quadrupeds*. Beilby wrote most of the text to accompany Bewick's illustrations and the first edition of *Quadrupeds* was published in 1790. Encouraged by this success, Bewick began work on another book looking at birds. Studying live birds or fresh specimens, while also taking inspiration from his own experiences observing the wildlife around him, his drawings were incredibly realistic and accurate. The *History of British Birds* was published in two volumes: *Land Birds* in 1797 and *Water Birds* in 1804.

The partnership with Beilby ended in 1798, but Bewick retained the engraving business and his skills were in great demand. Bewick continued working on commercial engraving projects as well as his books. He became especially well known for small decorative designs called 'vignettes' or 'tailpieces', used to fill an empty space at the bottom of a page. They were so popular that in 1827 Bewick published a book devoted entirely to these tiny masterpieces. At the suggestion of his daughter Jane, Bewick wrote his *Memoir*, beginning work on it in November 1822. It was completed on 1 November 1828, just seven days before he died aged 75. However, it was not published until 1862, and it has been suggested that this was because his religious and political views were controversial. The original manuscript is now in the collection of the British Museum, London.

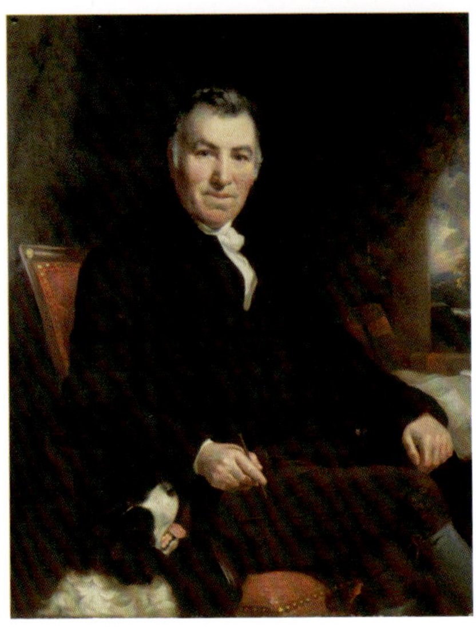

William Nicholson (1781–1844)
Portrait of Thomas Bewick,
exhibited 1814
Oil on canvas,
127.2 x 101.6 cm
Purchased 1951

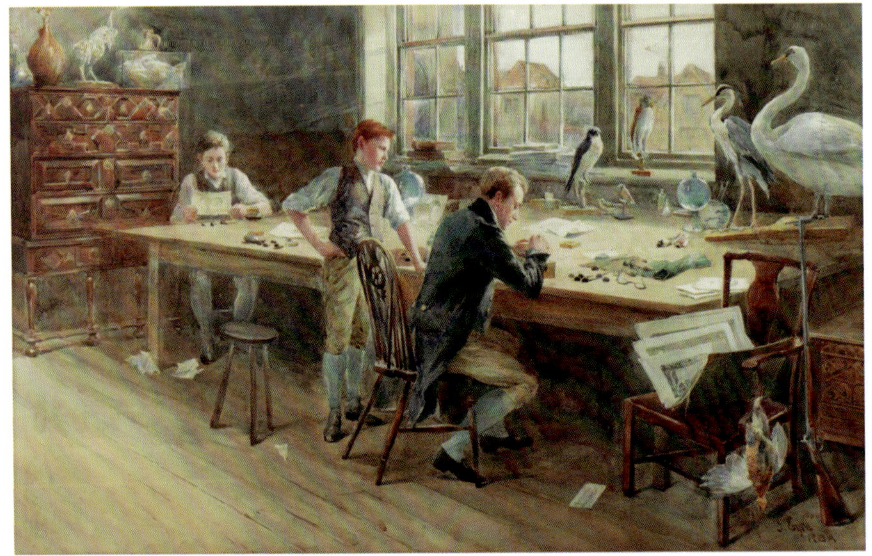

John Fyre (1850–1927)
The Master Engraver – Thomas Bewick in his Workshop, 1896
Watercolour, bodycolour and pencil on paper,
45.9 x 73.9 cm
Given by Mr Langwell, 1982

Here, Eyre has created an imaginary reconstruction of Bewick's workshop. Eyre had been shown the room at the workshop near St Nicholas's Churchyard while visiting Newcastle from London. Eyre's picture was exhibited at the Royal Society of British Artists in London, in 1896, and was later engraved for the *Illustrated London News*. This interest shows how famous Bewick remained many years after his death.

Below:
Thomas Bewick
The Reed Sparrow, before 1797
Watercolour, bodycolour and
pencil on paper, 17.5 x 21.7 cm
Given by Dr Croal Thompson,
1925

Right:
Thomas Bewick
**Printing block of the Eider duck
from *History of British Birds*,**
vol.2, 1800
Engraved wood, 5.5 x 8.1 x 2.2 cm
Given from a private collection,
1922

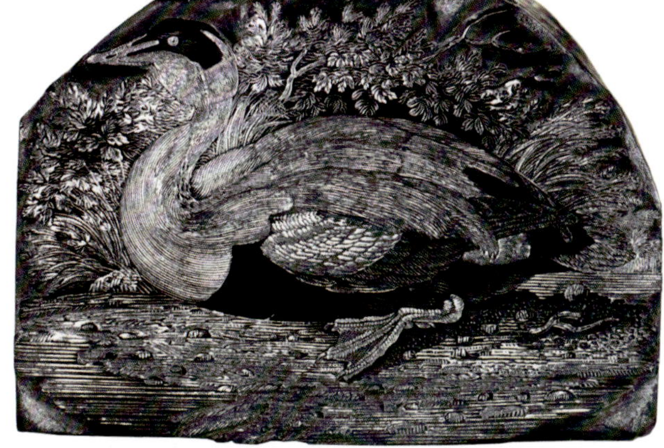

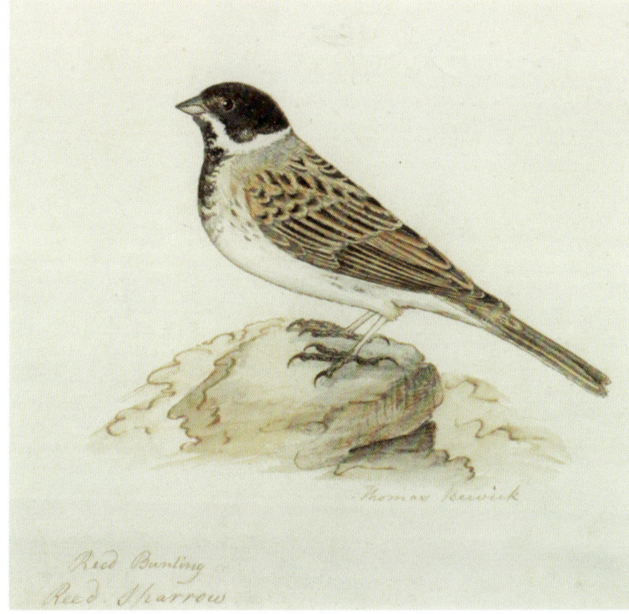

Below:
Thomas Bewick
The Hull, York and Newcastle Mail Coach, before 1807
Wood engraving, 17.4 x 41.8 cm
Purchased with grant aid from the Victoria and Albert Museum
Purchase Grant Fund and Friends of the Laing Art Gallery, 1982

This is an exceptionally large and fine wood-engraving by Bewick.
The coach is moving fast, the blinkered horses whipped on by the
coachman in order to keep to its strict timetable. The man sitting with
his back to the viewer is probably the armed guard who always
accompanied a mail coach. This particular print was owned by Bewick's
daughter Jane, who noted on the paper that the image was designed
and engraved by Thomas Bewick.

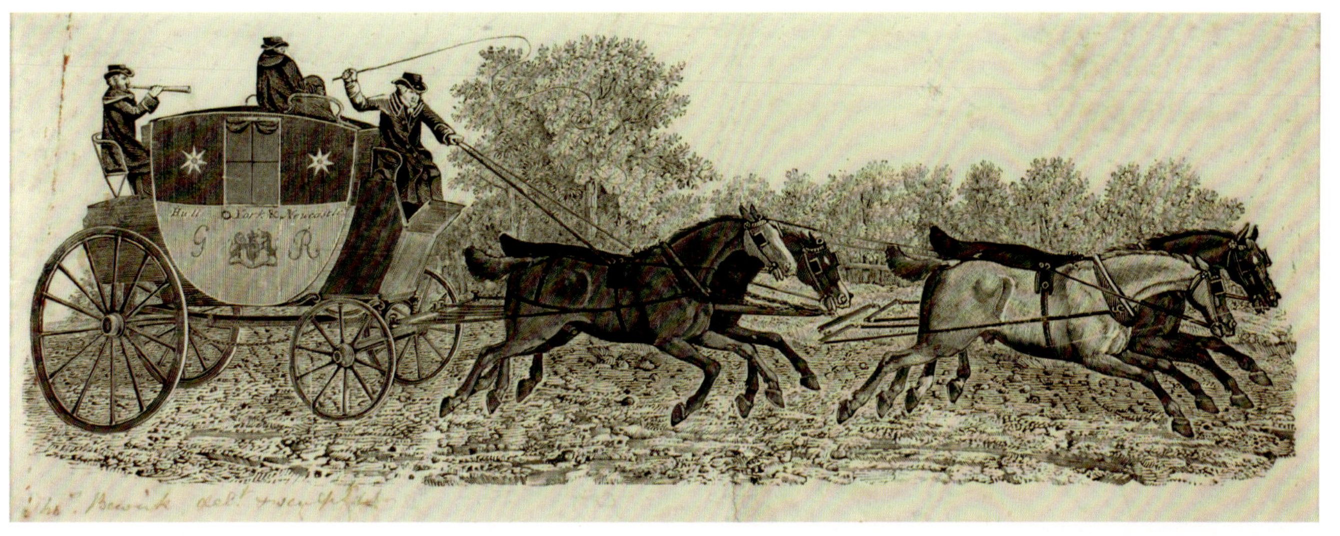

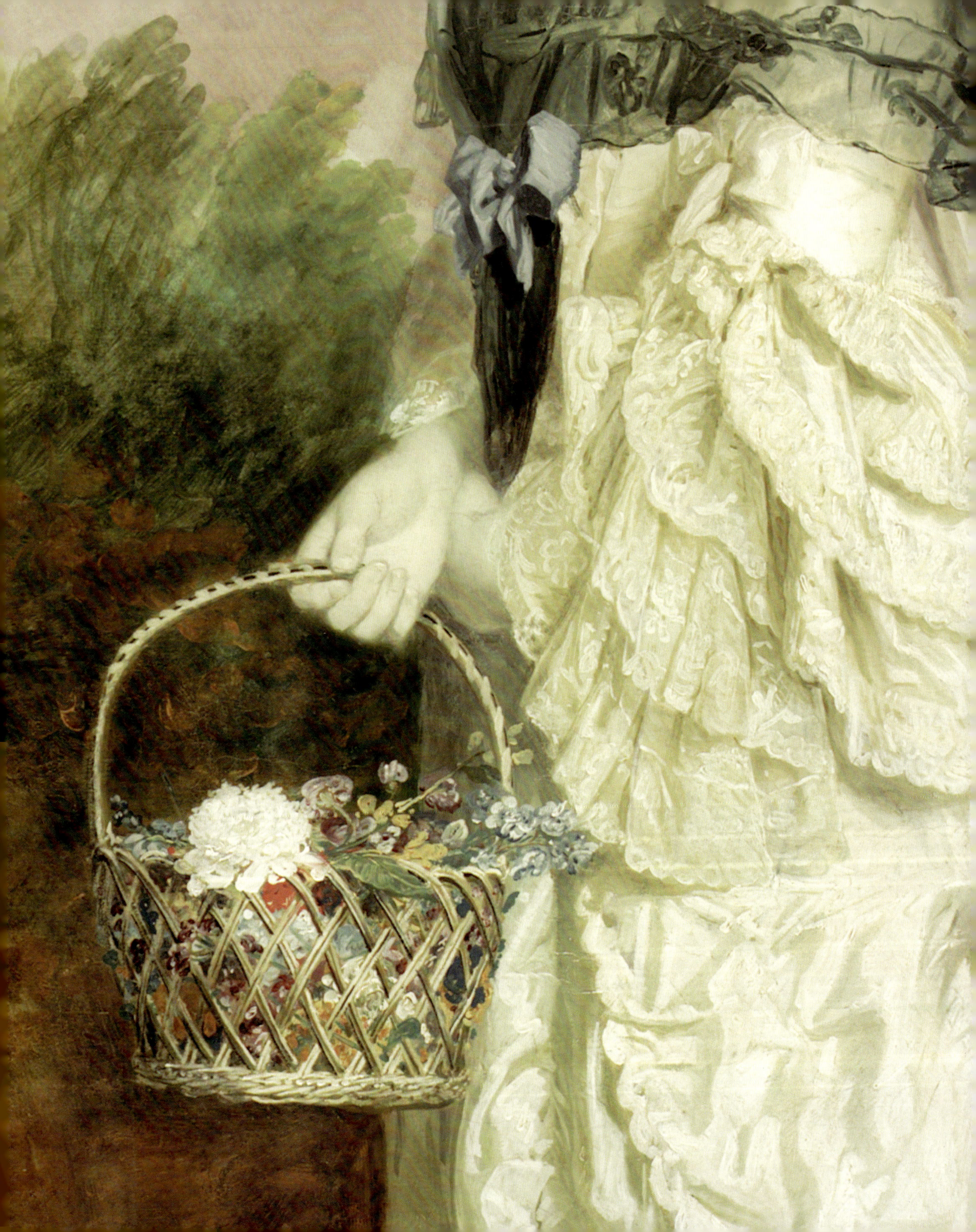

Sir Joshua Reynolds (1723–1792)
Portrait of Mrs Elizabeth Riddell, *c.*1760
Oil on canvas, 239 x 148.5 cm
Purchased with grant aid from the
Victoria and Albert Museum Purchase
Grant Fund, The Art Fund, James Knott
Fund and Pilgrim Trust, 1965

The Laing Art Gallery collection features
magnificent eighteenth-century portraits
by some of the most outstanding artists
of the day. At this time, artists such as
Sir Joshua Reynolds were developing a
more relaxed, natural style of portraiture,
contrasting with the traditional formality
of works by those such as Joseph Wright
of Derby.

Portrait of Mrs Elizabeth Riddell
illustrates the radical new approach to
portraiture that Reynolds introduced on
his return to England from Italy in 1752.
Mrs Riddell is posed in a natural way,
walking in what is perhaps her landscape
park at Swinburne Castle near Hexham,
where the portrait hung for nearly 200
years. The background has no draped
curtains or grand architecture, and is
quite sketchily painted, giving a much
lighter overall effect than earlier styles
used for large portraits. Remarkably,
Reynolds chose to place his sitter off-
centre in the scene, to create a sense of
movement. Mrs Riddell wears a highly
fashionable contemporary rococo dress
in ruched ivory satin, rather than the kind
of fantasy costume that had previously
been popular in portraits. However
elaborate the dress may appear to us
today, it would have been regarded by
wealthy contemporaries as suitable for
wear in this country setting. Mrs Riddell's
pale complexion is the result of Reynolds
having used rosy glazes for her skin,
which have since faded.

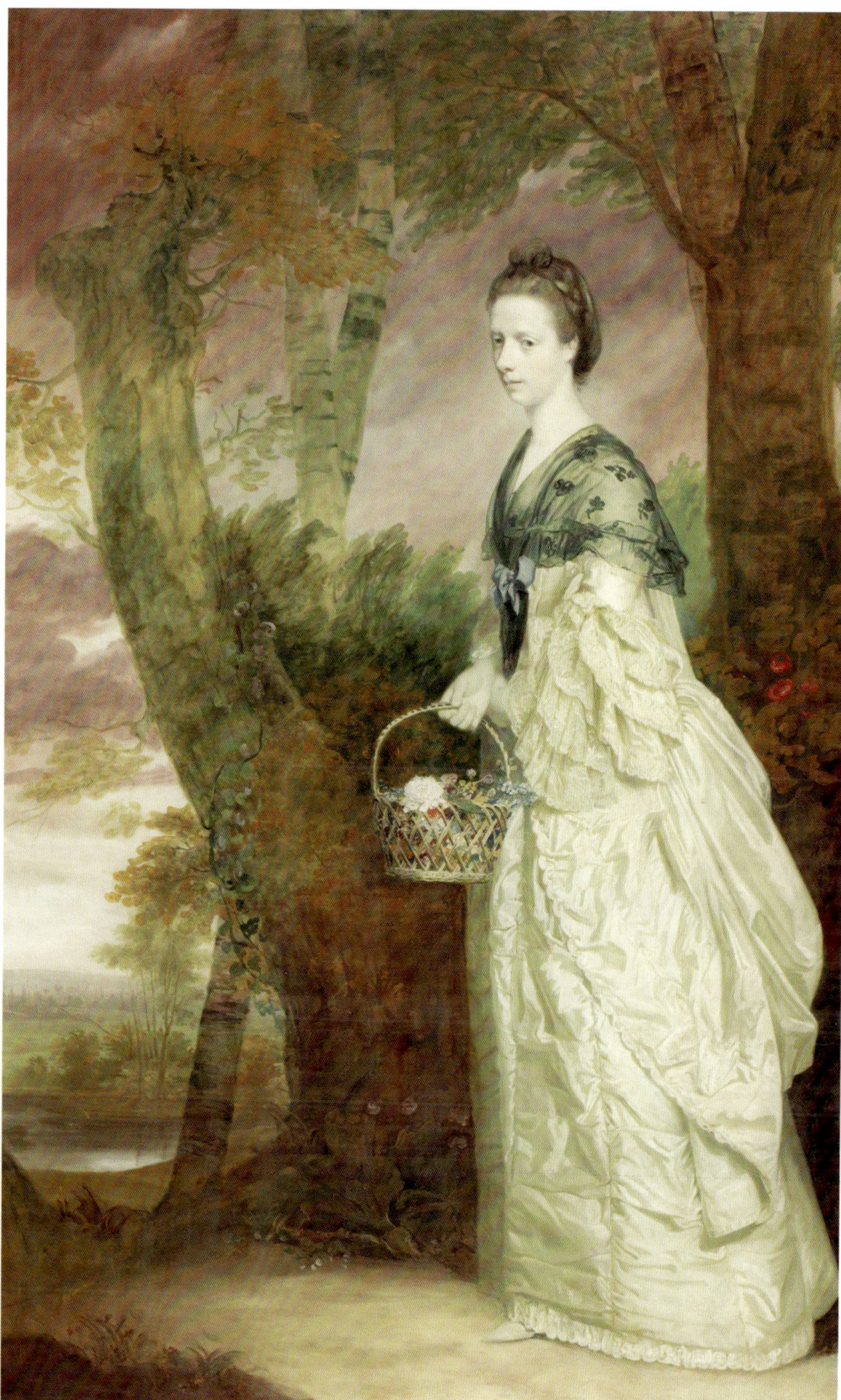

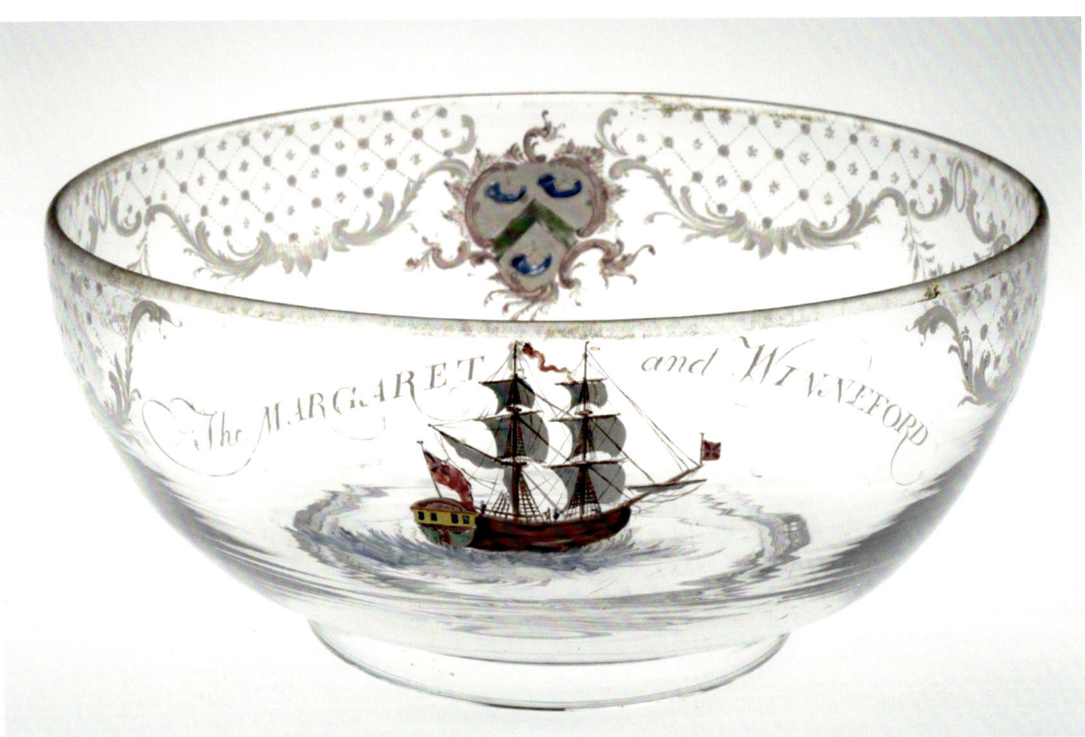

Attributed to William Beilby (1740–1819)
The Margaret and Winneford Bowl, *c.*1767
Glass with painted enamel decoration and gilding,
10.7 x 24.1 cm
Purchased with grant aid from the Victoria and Albert Museum
Purchase Grant Fund, The Art Fund, The National Heritage
Memorial Fund, the Worshipful Company of Glass Sellers, Tyne
and Wear County Council, Friends of the Laing Art Gallery,
Sqn Ldr J. Rush and via public appeal, 1985

The Beilbys were a family of Newcastle craftspeople who had
a workshop at Amen Corner, near St Nicholas's Churchyard.
They worked in many crafts, including decorating silver and
glass, and printing. However, they are especially known for
their glass painted with enamel colours. On the Continent the
technique of glass enamelling was well established, but William
Beilby was the first British maker to master the technique of
firing enamel onto glass to fix it. Using this method, he was
able to paint strong colours and fancy designs onto goblets,
bowls and other glassware. William taught his brothers Ralph
and Thomas and his sister Mary, and together the family
decorated locally made glass. It is unlikely that Beilby glass was
produced after 1767, when William became a drawing master.
Signed pieces of Beilby glass are very rare and other craftsmen
produced similar decoration.

The *Margaret and Winneford* was the first ship to be built
on Hillgate Quay in Gateshead. Named after his two daughters,
it was launched by the Admiral of the Fleet, Sir John Forster, on
13 April 1767. To commemorate the launching, William Beilby
was commissioned to produce this bowl, to be presented to
the Admiral. A view of the ship in full sail is painted on the
front of the bowl. On the back is the coat of arms of the Forster
family of Bamburgh, Northumberland. Inside, on the base, is a
magnificent white swan (see below). This is the only known
example of Beilby glass to feature this kind of decoration and it
may have been placed there to disguise the pontil mark, a stub
of glass left on the base where the glass-blowing pipe was
broken off.

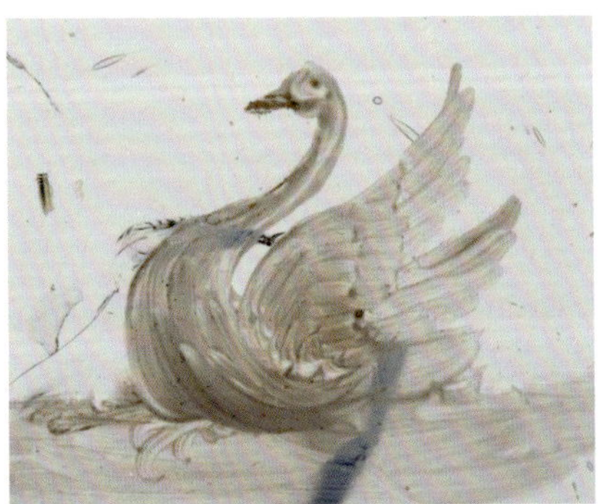

Sowerby Art Glass Studio (1870–1888)
Opalescent Glass Vase, *c.*1885
Free-blown glass, 17.6 x 14 cm
Given by Misses C. & T. Baumgartner,
1973

The Sowerby family were glassmakers
from around 1760, although they did
not establish their Sowerby Glassworks
in Gateshead until 1807. During the next
150 years their trademark peacock's
head became known as a mark of quality.
An Art Glass Studio was established at
Sowerby's Ellison Glassworks in about
1870 and continued in production until
around 1888. This was in response to an
increased interest in older glassmaking
techniques such as hand-blowing, and
the fashion for Venetian-style glass of
the sixteenth and seventeenth centuries.
Sowerby's brought in a group of expert
glassmakers from Murano in Italy to work
at the studio, who taught their techniques
to the Gateshead glassworkers.

The art glass made at the studio was
not widely advertised, although it often
featured in trade exhibitions as an
example of the quality of Sowerby glass.
The glass was not mass-produced, each
piece being unique. The last recorded
mention of Sowerby Art Glass was in
1885, when it appeared in showroom
exhibitions in Bond Street and Oxford
Street, London. This opalescent glass
vase dates from around that time and
is typical of the work the Studio was
producing – a blown glass vessel with
pincered and crimped decorations
applied. Opalescent glass is so called
because of its resemblance to the opal
gemstone and is often iridescent,
producing rainbow colours. Sowerby's
made this subtle bluish glass, naming it
'Opal'. The shimmering finish was a
modern development at the time. The
overall design of the piece works well
with 'opal' glass, demonstrating the way
in which levels of transparency vary
according to the thickness of the glass.

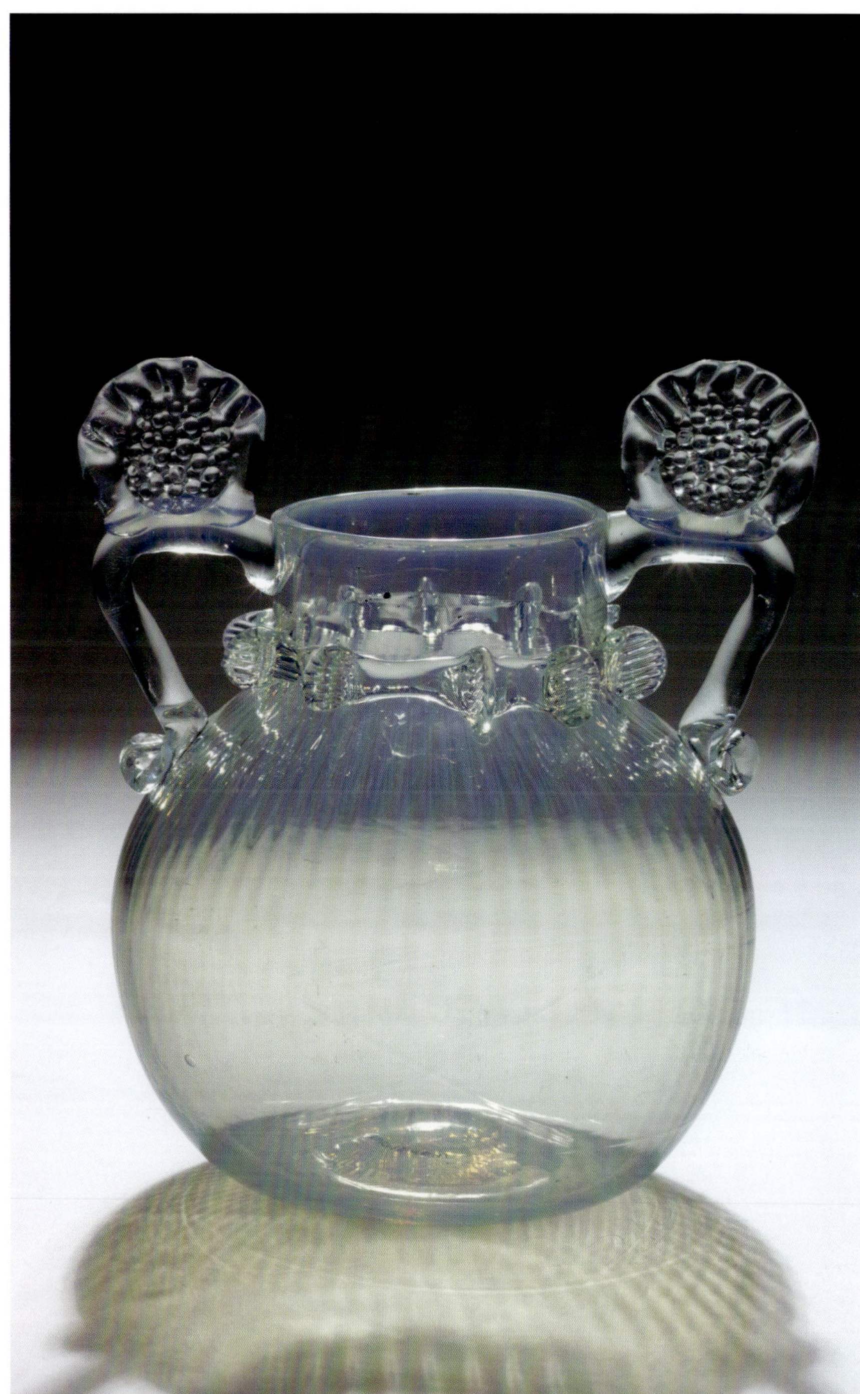

John Martin (1789–1854)

John Martin was one of the best-known artists of his generation. He was born into a large and loving but very poor family living at East Landends, near Haydon Bridge in Northumberland. His imagination was fired by the beautiful and dramatic countryside around him and also by the powerful Old Testament Bible stories his mother told to her children. Hoping to help their son's artistic ambitions, the family moved to Newcastle when John was 14. He trained with a coachbuilder for a year to learn heraldry painting and studied for another year with a drawing teacher. Apart from that, however, he was self-taught. He moved to London at the age of 17, where he got a job painting designs on ceramics. He had no influential connections and little money, but he worked at his art until he was able to display paintings at London exhibitions.

Over time, Martin developed his individual interpretation of Romantic 'Sublime' art. His importance is due to the new style he created, combining enormously exaggerated landscape and architectural settings with masses of tiny figures, and using powerful colours and dramatic light effects. People were enthralled by these exciting images and barriers sometimes had to be put up to keep the crowds back at exhibitions. His most famous pictures were scenes of crisis and destruction illustrating Bible stories and subjects from poems. However, the theatricality of his pictures was often attacked by art reviewers.

Martin's fame was spread by his extremely accomplished mezzotint prints, which enabled many ordinary people in Britain and abroad to own examples of his art. Unfortunately, he made some poor business decisions over his prints.

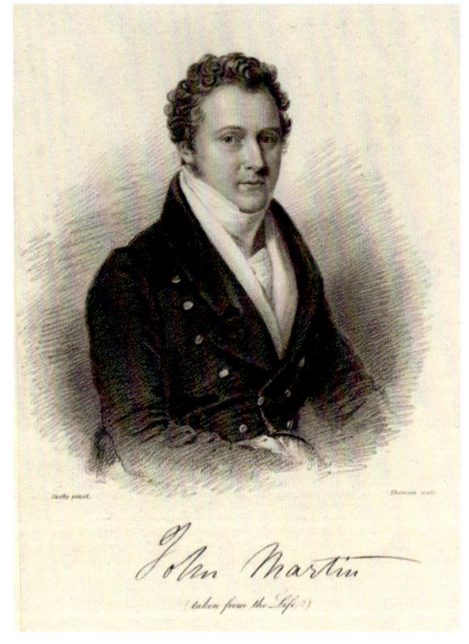

Engraved by James Thompson (1789–1850), after William Derby (1786–1847)
John Martin (taken from the Life), published 1822
Stipple engraving
Acquired 1981
TWCMS: F4765

At the same time, he became fixated on designing engineering schemes for London, mainly concerning improvement of the water supply, which came to nothing. As a result, his career suffered until he returned to painting the kind of huge, dramatic scenes that had first made him famous. However, tastes in art were changing and Martin was becoming unfashionable even before his death. In 1935, his masterpieces, the three immense *Last Judgement* canvases now in Tate Britain, were sold for only £7. But interest in Martin revived soon after the Second World War, largely due to the collectors Robert and Charlotte Frank. The Laing Art Gallery's own collection of 16 oil paintings and watercolours by Martin contains eight works from the Franks's collection, purchased in 1976. It is now the largest and most representative collection of Martin's extraordinary work.

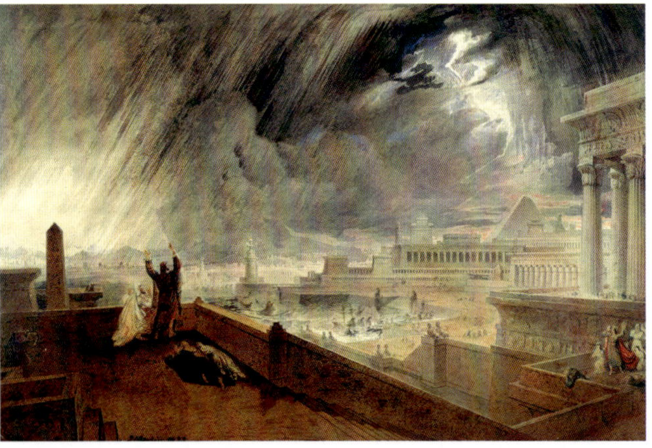

John Martin
Design for the *Seventh Plague of Egypt*, 1823
Watercolour and ink on paper, 24.5 x 37 cm
Purchased with grant aid from the Victoria and Albert Museum Purchase Grant Fund, The Art Fund and Pilgrim Trust, 1976

This very detailed watercolour is characteristic of the subjects that made Martin famous, although its tiny size contrasts with the huge scale of his best-known oil paintings. The picture illustrates the 'Seventh Plague of Egypt' described in the Book of Exodus in the Bible. Moses, on the left, stretches up his staff to heaven, calling down thunder, hail and fire. The Egyptian fleet in the harbour is being swamped by the storm. Martin used illustrations of archaeological excavations to provide details for the impressive buildings bordering the harbour.

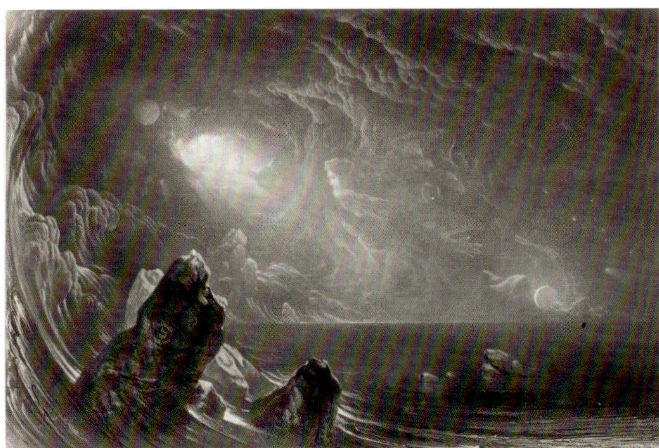

Above:
John Martin
The Creation, published 1839
Mezzotint etching, 26.8 x 35.4 cm
Purchased 1945

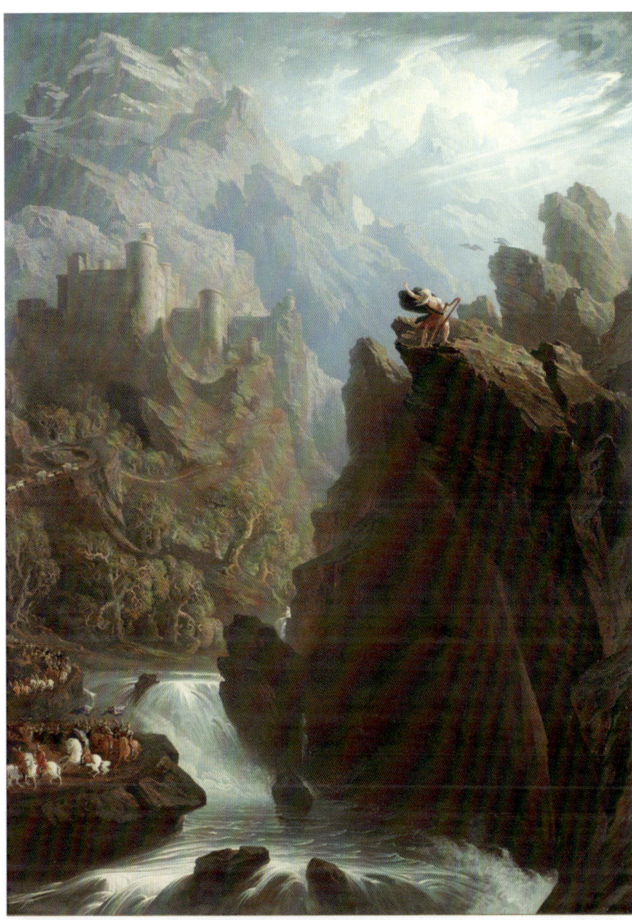

Right:
John Martin
The Bard, exhibited 1817
Oil on canvas, 215.5 x 157 cm
Purchased with grant aid from
The Art Fund, 1951

This painting illustrates Thomas
Gray's poem of the same name,
which described the
(subsequently discredited) story
of the destruction of the Welsh
bards by King Edward I in the
thirteenth century. The subject
was a popular one with artists of
the Romantic period.

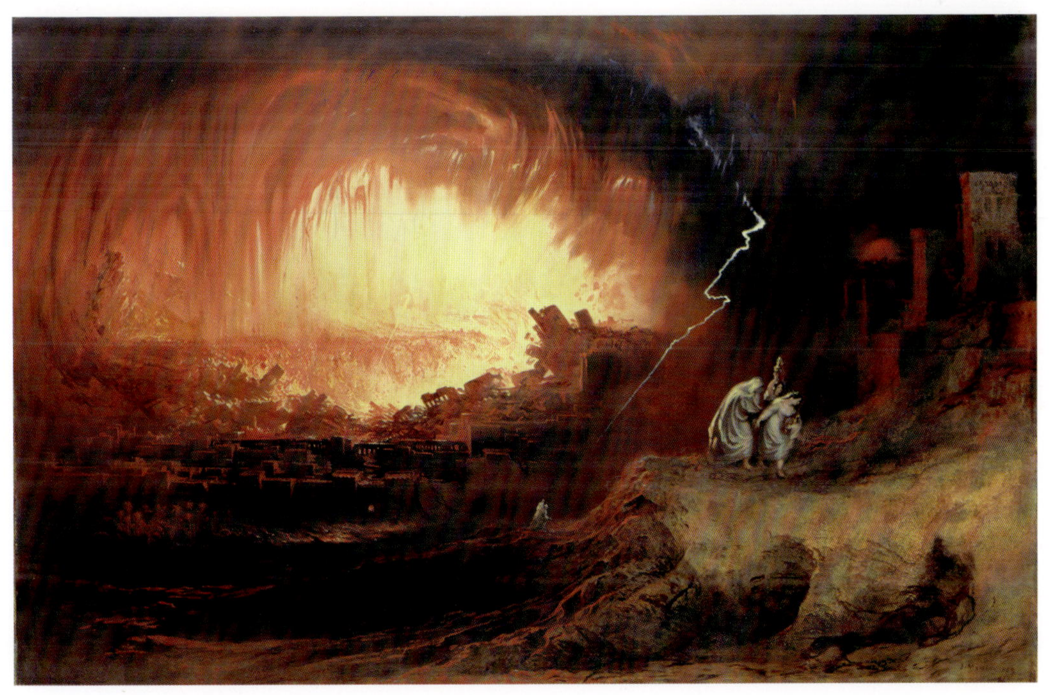

Left:
John Martin
*The Destruction of
Sodom and Gomorrah*,
1852
Oil on canvas,
136.3 x 212.3 cm
Given by E.F. Weidner,
Esq., and his co-Trustees,
in memory of the late
John Frederick Weidner,
JP, Lord Mayor of
Newcastle (1912–13), 1951

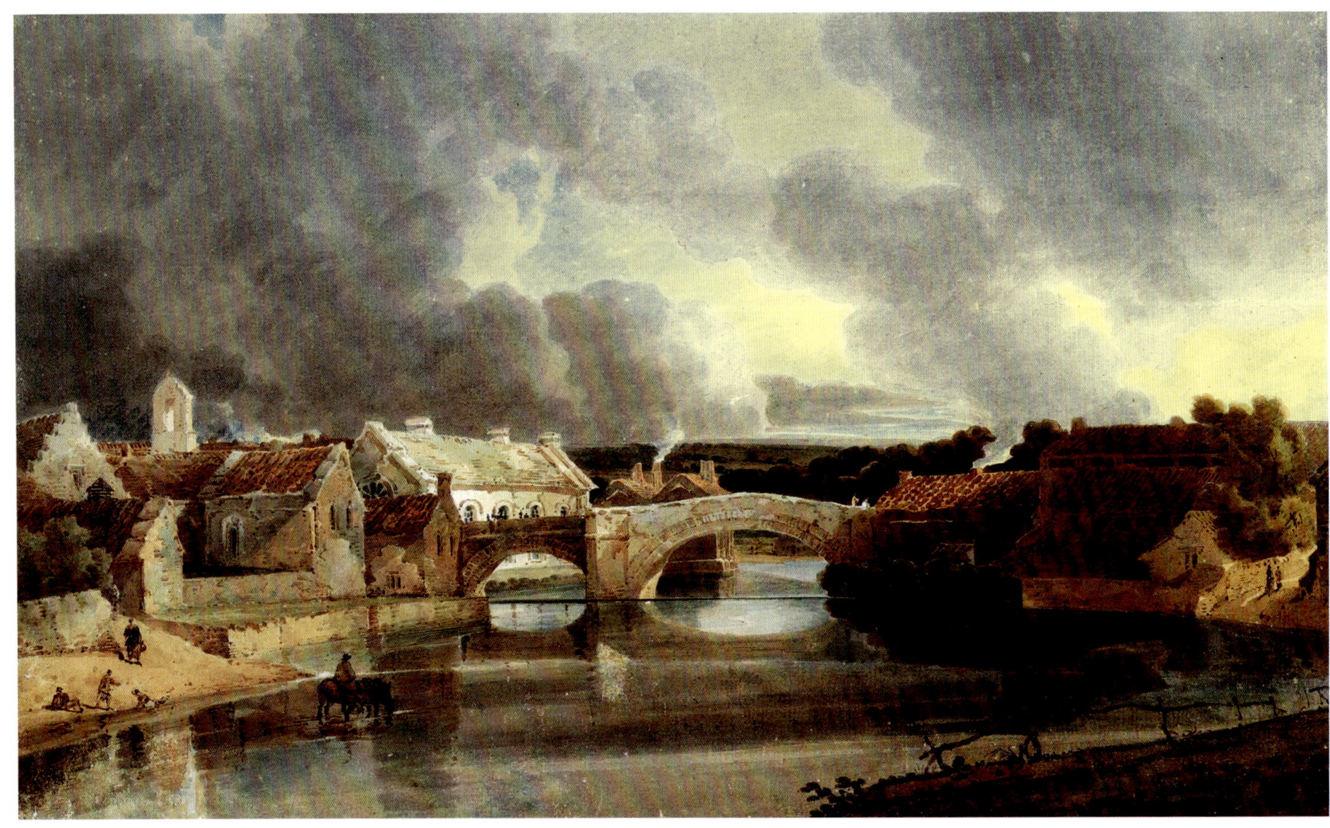

Thomas Girtin (1775–1802)
Morpeth Bridge, *c*.1802
Watercolour, ink and pencil on paper, 32.1 x 52.9 cm
Purchased with grant aid from the Victoria and Albert Museum
Purchase Grant Fund, Trustees of the John Wigham Richardson
Bequest, The Art Fund and Friends of the Laing Art Gallery, 1979

The main strengths of the Laing's watercolour collection lie in
the eighteenth- and nineteenth-century works, when ground-
breaking developments took place in British watercolours,
especially in landscape painting. Previously, artists had used
the medium to create outline drawings with grey shading, but
with improvements in paper quality and the range of colours
available, they became more experimental. They were skilled at
allowing the white paper to shine through transparent washes
of colour, producing sensations of light and atmosphere.

Thomas Girtin was influenced by the work of earlier artists
such as John Robert Cozens, but developed ways of working
with watercolour beyond anything done previously. Girtin did
not use a preliminary grey wash shading, thereby giving a
brighter and more naturalistic effect. The paintings were built
up in a series of luminous thin layers or washes of colour, creating powerful, bold compositions, full of light and atmosphere.
He painted this view of Morpeth Bridge from sketches made
during an extended tour of Northumberland in 1800. He used
thick, slightly rough paper, its texture breaking up the colour
and helping to produce a sense of air and weather. With great
skill, bare paper has been left for the two tiny figures on the
bridge. There is very little pencil drawing and Girtin applied
the harmonious gold, brown and grey watercolour washes
quite freely.

Sadly, Girtin died when he was only 27, shortly after painting
Morpeth Bridge. His friend and fellow student J.M.W. Turner
acknowledged his greatness when he later said, 'Had Tom
Girtin lived, I should have starved' (W. Thornbury, *The Life of
J.M.W. Turner, R.A.*, London, 1862, vol.i, p.117).

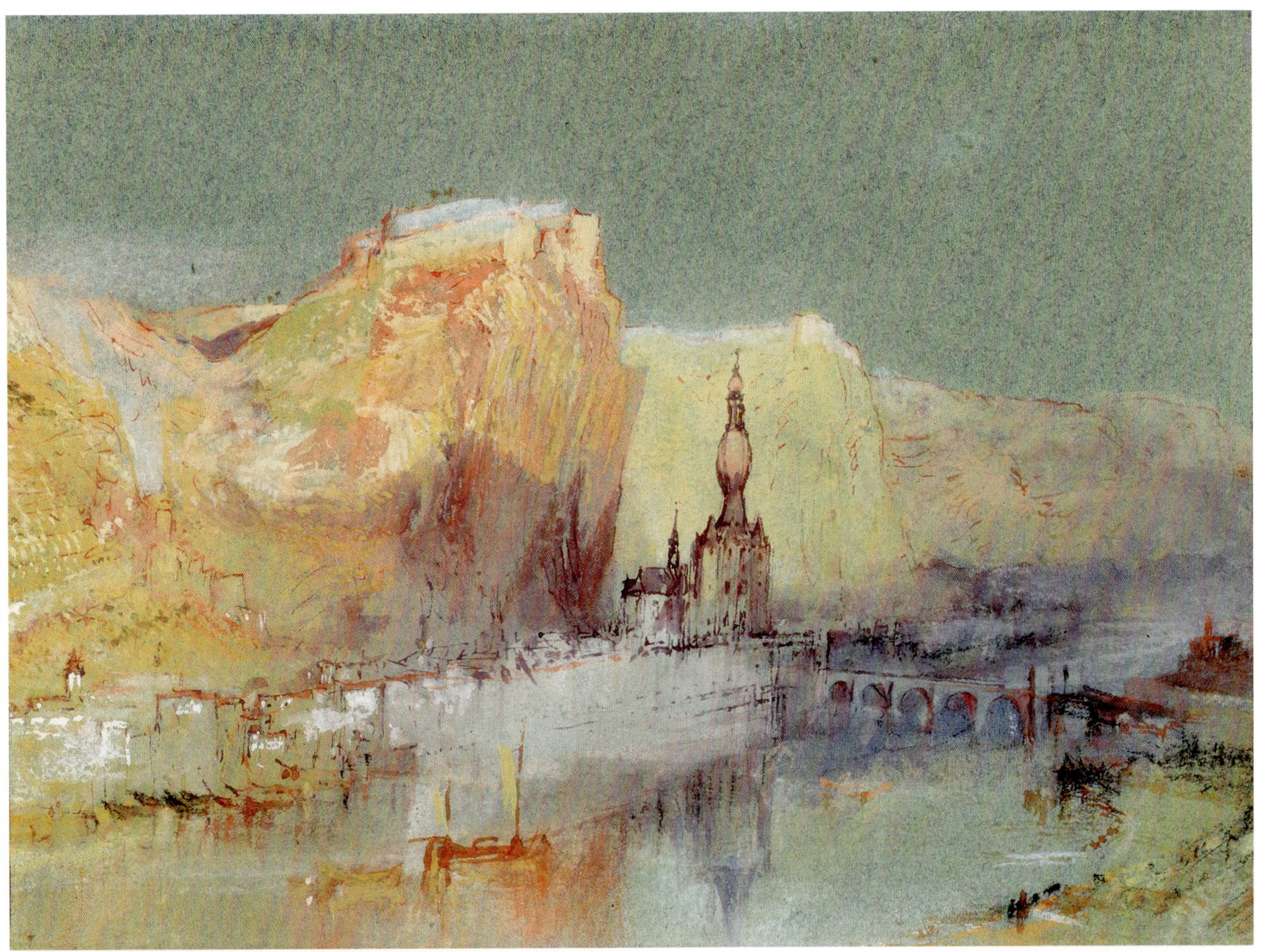

Joseph Mallord William Turner (1775–1851)
Dinant sur Meuse, 1839
Watercolour, bodycolour, pencil and chalk on paper,
13.6 x 18.8 cm
Given by John Wigham Richardson, 1925

During the late eighteenth and early nineteenth centuries, many artists began exploring nature in a much more realistic way than they had done before. They started working in the open air, taking their sketching equipment out into the countryside. Formal compositions gradually gave way to naturalistic landscape scenes, and as artists travelled widely in search of dramatic and attractive views, scenes of faraway places became particularly popular in the nineteenth century.

An example of such an artist was Joseph Mallord William Turner, considered one of the greatest British landscape painters. He became an Associate of the Royal Academy at the age of 24, and a full member two years later in 1802, when he was 26 – the youngest member to be received. He is perhaps best known for his oil paintings, but Turner also produced a large number of watercolour paintings throughout his working life. On his death, over 19,000 drawings and watercolours were bequeathed to the nation, now housed at Tate Britain, and not including works in other collections. As well as working in Britain, he travelled extensively throughout Europe, particularly France, Switzerland and Italy.

In the 1830s Turner often sketched on blue paper, torn into pocket-sized pieces. He used this method for *Dinant sur Meuse,* painted during his tour of the Rivers Meuse and Mosel in 1839. One of several studies of dramatic rock formations, it is painted in opaque watercolour after a pencil sketch made on the spot. Turner was probably planning to follow up his earlier successful series of prints of the rivers of France. However, this particular sketch was not reproduced as an engraving. It once belonged to Turner's champion, the Victorian art critic John Ruskin.

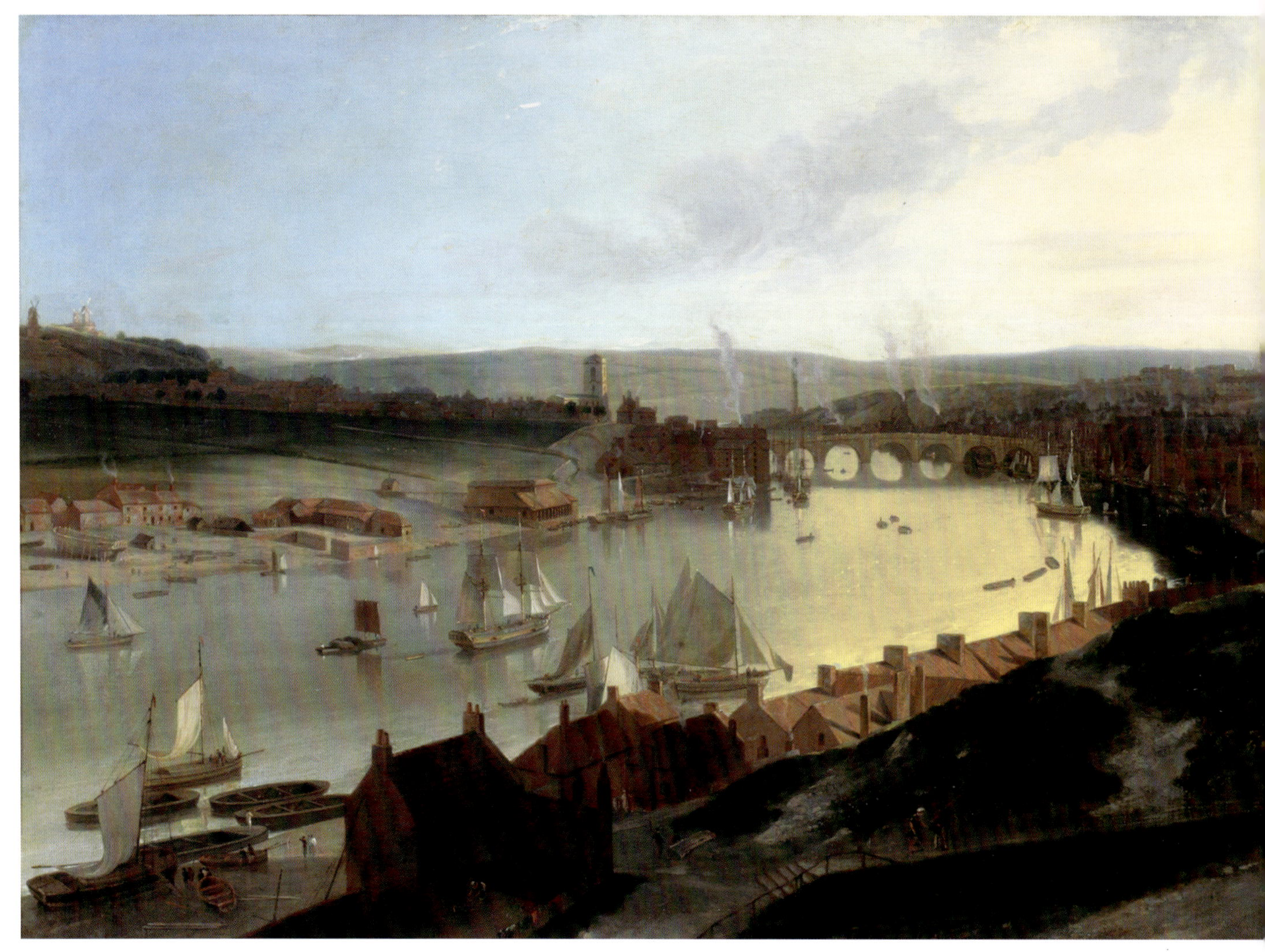

William Daniell (1769–1837)
View of Newcastle upon Tyne, taken from a windmill to the eastward of St Ann's, *c.*1802–3
Oil on canvas, 95.3 x 186 cm
Purchased with grant aid from the Victoria and Albert Museum Purchase Grant Fund, The Art Fund, Friends of the Laing Art Gallery and The Business Partners Fund, 2005

William Daniell was a London painter, watercolourist and engraver who travelled extensively throughout the British Isles. He is best known for his topographical and architectural subjects, and he painted many port and coast views, becoming skilled at depicting ships as well as the surrounding buildings. He often took a high, bird's-eye viewpoint, achieving detailed panoramas, in contrast to many artists who chose water-level views to accentuate imposing riverside buildings.

From 1801 to 1803, Daniell made a tour of the north of Britain. During this time he made studies for *View of Newcastle upon Tyne, taken from a windmill to the eastward of St Ann's*, which was exhibited at the Royal Academy in 1804. The painting shows the famous medieval Tyne Bridge spanning the middle distance. Key landmarks include All Saints' Church, Newcastle, the medieval St Nicholas's Church (later Cathedral), and the Norman castle that gave Newcastle its name. The details of the picture provide an important record of Tyneside industry at the beginning of the nineteenth century. On a sandy path on the right a horse-drawn coal wagon is coming down to the Tyne, taking its load to the coal keels (barges) and sea-

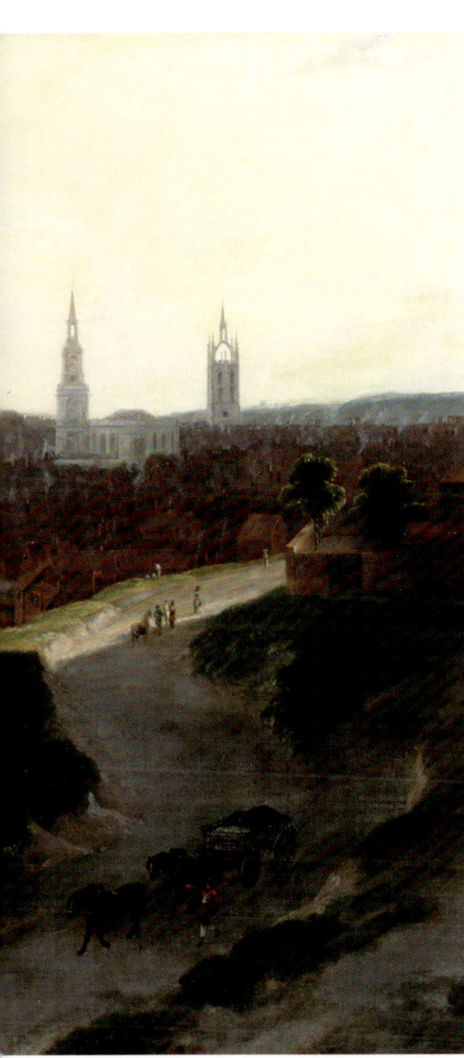

Edward Montgomery O'Rourke Dickey
(1894–1977)
The Building of the Tyne Bridge, 1928
Oil on canvas, 101.7 x 76.2 cm
Purchased 1929

The bridges across the Tyne have helped give the city of Newcastle its identity for hundreds of years, but perhaps most iconic of all is the Tyne Bridge. Built by Dorman, Long & Company of Middlesbrough, which also constructed the similar Sydney Harbour Bridge in Australia, the Tyne Bridge was opened in 1928 by King George V.

This painting shows the later stages of the bridge's construction. The soaring arch spanning the river is almost complete, while sections of the roadway suspended from it are being swung into place by cranes. Like many pictures of this period, it is painted in a limited range of pale colours, emphasising line and pattern. Patches of light blue over dark green re-create reflections on the surface of the river. Edward Dickey was Director of the School of Art in Newcastle from 1926 to 1931. This was an outpost of Durham University at the time and later became part of Newcastle University. Dickey displayed this painting at the 1928–29 New English Art Club exhibition in London. He was also a skilled wood-engraver and a founder member of the Society of Wood Engravers, illustrating a number of books and showing several works in their exhibitions.

going coal ships on the river. On the Gateshead bank, a coal wagonway runs down to a huge store and loading staith (wharf). Shipbuilding is represented with two ships being fitted in a boat-builders' yard on the Newcastle bank, and another ship under construction on the Gateshead bank. A forest of masts on the Newcastle side near the bridge shows the location of the main commercial quay, and in the distance on the far left are the corn-grinding windmills on Windmills Hill, Gateshead.

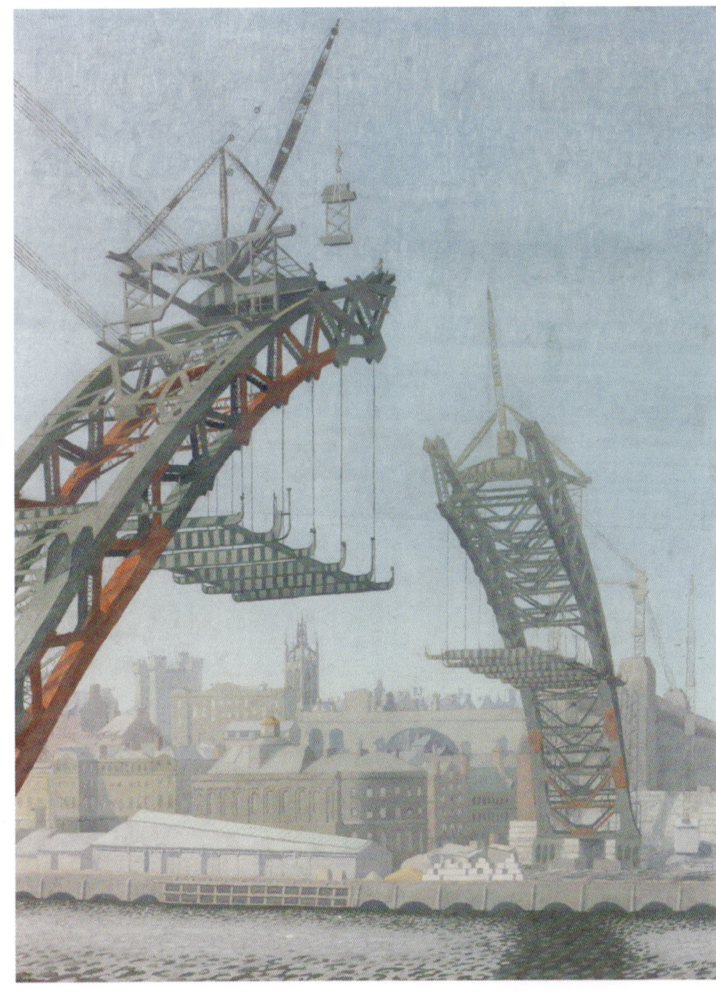

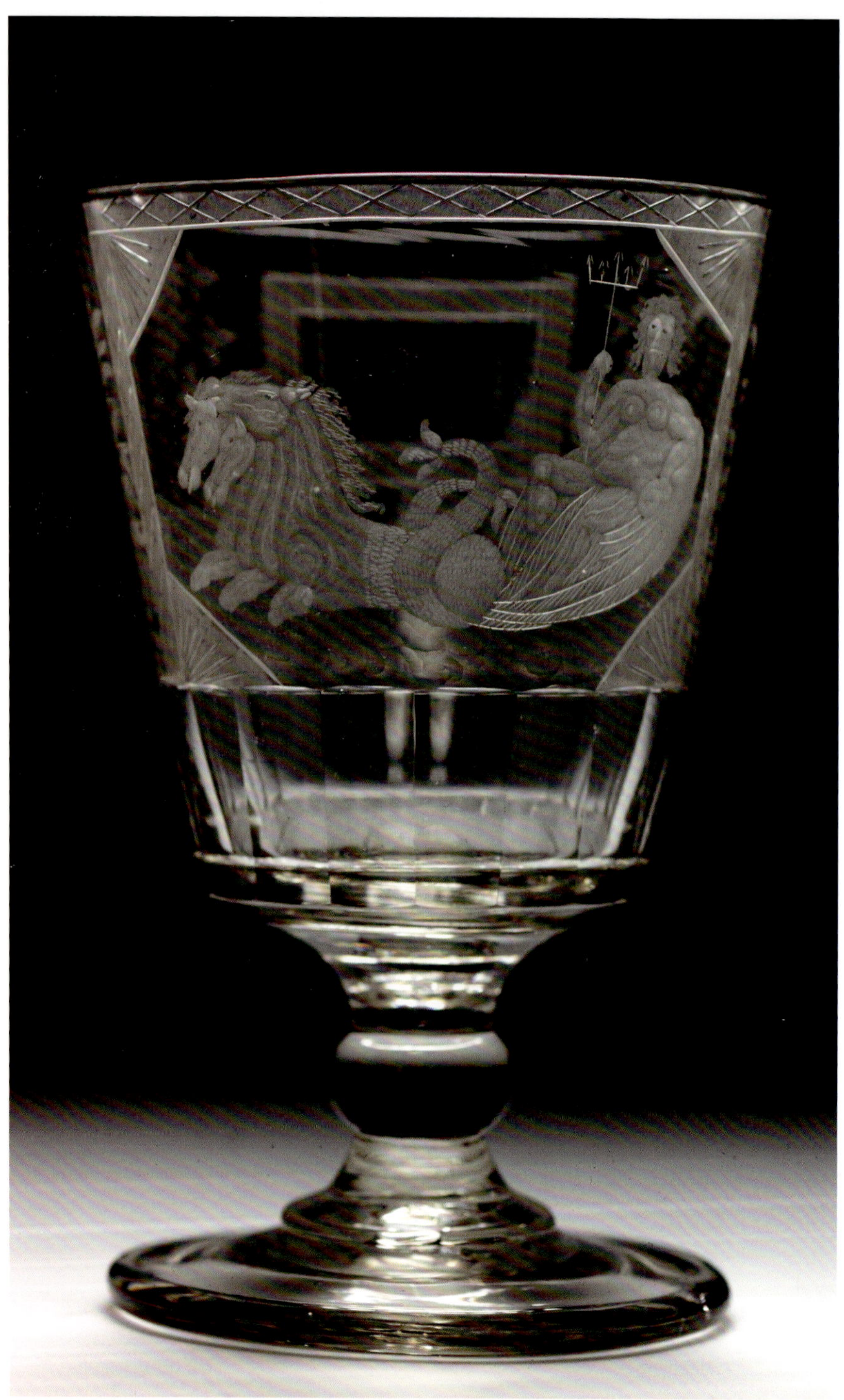

Newcastle glass, engraved by Thomas Hudson (nineteenth century)
'Neptune' Goblet, *c*.1840
Glass, 23.1 x 15.3 cm
Purchased 1929

During the eighteenth century Newcastle was the largest glass-producing centre in the world. Its location was ideal, with plentiful raw materials, coal for the furnaces and the River Tyne for exporting finished goods. The industry grew up around the Skinnerburn and the Ouseburn, and by 1827 there were 41 glasshouses working in the area. Newcastle glass was considered to be very high quality and much of it was exported to Europe, especially to the Netherlands where the most skilled engravers worked. Once engraved, the glass was frequently imported back to England for sale.

Glass engravers were working on Tyneside in the eighteenth century, but it was not until the early nineteenth century that the technique became well established. The main local engraver was Robert Hudson who in 1806 advertised his skill with 'coats of arms, crests, cyphers or any other devices, engraved on flint glass in the neatest manner' (*Newcastle Courant*, 17 May 1806). Robert's son, Thomas Hudson, continued in his father's profession.

The 'Neptune' goblet is signed 'T. Hudson Newcastle'. Straight-sided, bucket-shaped goblets such as this are also called 'rummers' after 'römer', a type of German wine glass. The shape was particularly good for engraving on. It is decorated with a picture of the Roman god Neptune, king of the sea, riding in a chariot drawn by mythological creatures called hippocampi. A hippocampus has the head and forelegs of a horse and the tail of a dolphin.

Newcastle Handicrafts Company
Mermaid Cup and Cover, 1902
Silver with enamelled decoration,
28.3 x 12 cm
Purchased with grant aid from the
Victoria and Albert Museum Purchase
Grant Fund, Gateshead Acquisitions
Fund and Friends of the Laing Art
Gallery, 1997

The Goldsmiths' Company of Newcastle
was founded in 1716, and throughout the
eighteenth century increasing merchant
and industrial wealth created a growing
demand for luxury goods, with more
and more goldsmiths setting themselves
up in business on Tyneside. The area of
Newcastle around The Side became the
centre of the silver industry. While the
Newcastle Assay Office closed in 1884,
craftsmen continued to work in the area.

The Newcastle Handicrafts Company
was established in 1899 by Newcastle's
Art Committee. It was set up to promote
the teaching, production and commercial
distribution of the decorative arts, and
specialised in embroidery, enamel, wood-
work and metalwork. The Company was
placed under the supervision of Richard
Hatton, the headmaster and art teacher
at the College of Physical Science,
Newcastle, and became a significant
workshop within the Arts and Crafts
Movement until it ceased trading in 1912.

The mermaid cup and cover was
designed for the Company by Hatton
in 1902. Based on traditional styles of
ecclesiastical silver chalices, it is
decorated with three enamelled plaques
depicting Art Nouveau mermaids in a
background of waves tinged with
purple and green enamel. These were
the colours of the Women's Suffrage
Movement, with which the original
owners of the cup, Dr Ethel Williams
and Dr Ethel Bentham, were involved.
They became Founders of the Medical
Women's Federation in 1917 and worked
to improve medical care for women and
children, both regionally and nationally.

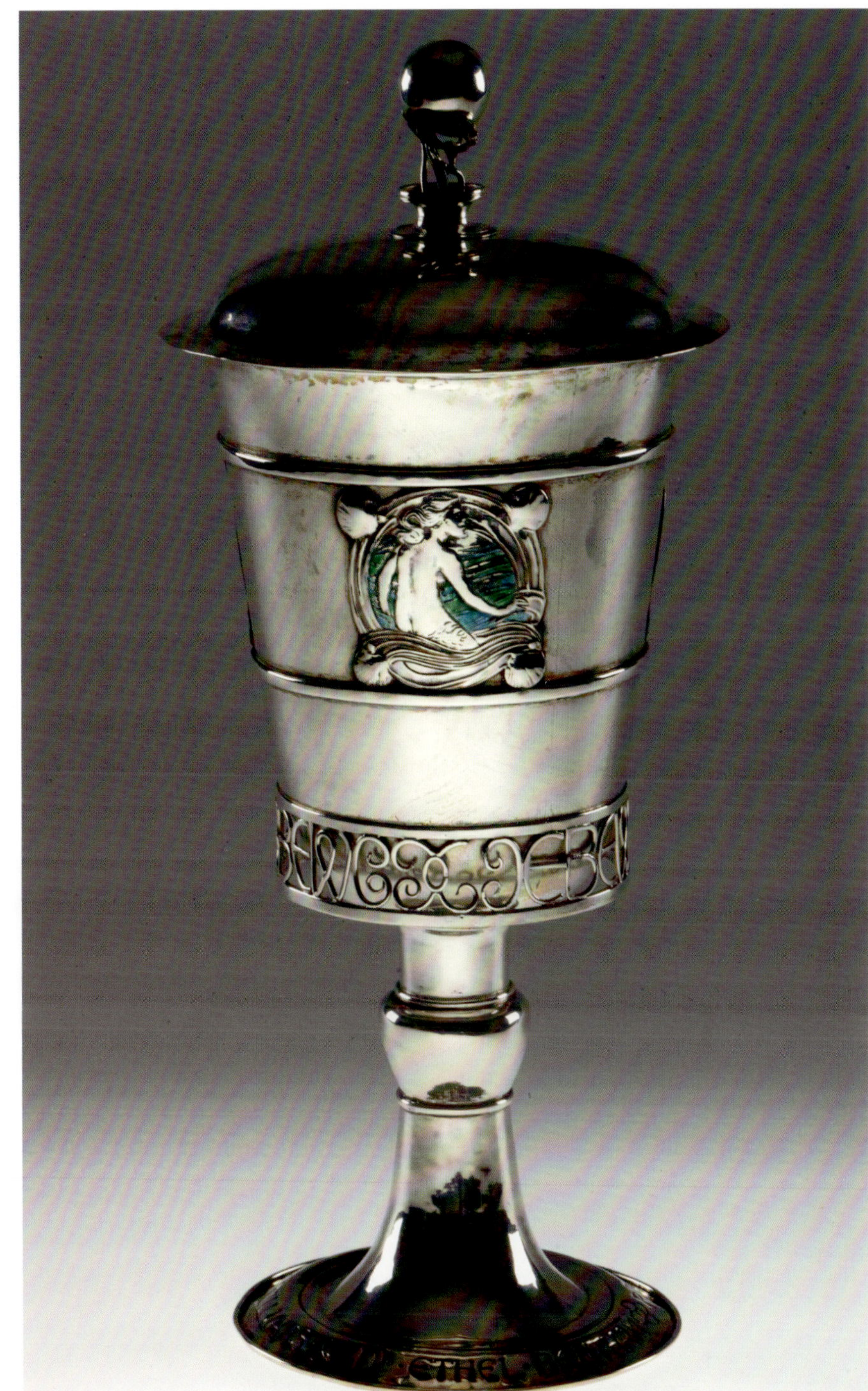

Ralph Hedley (1848–1913)

At the beginning of the twentieth century, Ralph Hedley was the major artist of Tyneside. His work was exhibited regularly and successfully in London, and was extremely popular on Tyneside, where he became a well-known public figure. His pictures of the daily lives of working people in the North East of England are typical of the Victorian Realist style, and an important contribution to the culture of the northern region.

Hedley first began exhibiting his paintings in 1878 in Newcastle. The next year he started showing his pictures in London. A popular and successful artist, Hedley ran a busy woodcarving workshop, which supplied fittings for many churches, including Newcastle Cathedral. He was also one of the key people attempting to establish Newcastle as a regional centre for painting. He was a founding member of the Newcastle Life School in 1878 and a Vice-President at the inception in 1883 of the influential society of northern artists, the Bewick Club.

Hedley believed that 'an artist should give special study to events of our own day in preference to those which took place say a couple of centuries ago', and set himself the task of recording life in the north of England in his paintings ('The Bewick Club and its founders – Ralph Hedley', *The Monthly Chronicle of North Country Lore and Legend*, vol.3, no.27, May 1889, p.197). Scenes such as *Going Home* (1888), showing miners coming off shift, were widely reproduced as prints, and it was said that no working man's home was considered complete without a framed copy of this or another of Hedley's prints of working life on the wall. He also painted light-hearted school scenes and charming views of North East cottage life. In the 1880s Hedley began to paint in the open air, moving out of the studio. He also experimented with different effects of light in interior scenes. Today, the Laing Art Gallery has the most extensive public collection of pictures by Hedley and he remains one of the best-loved artists in the collection.

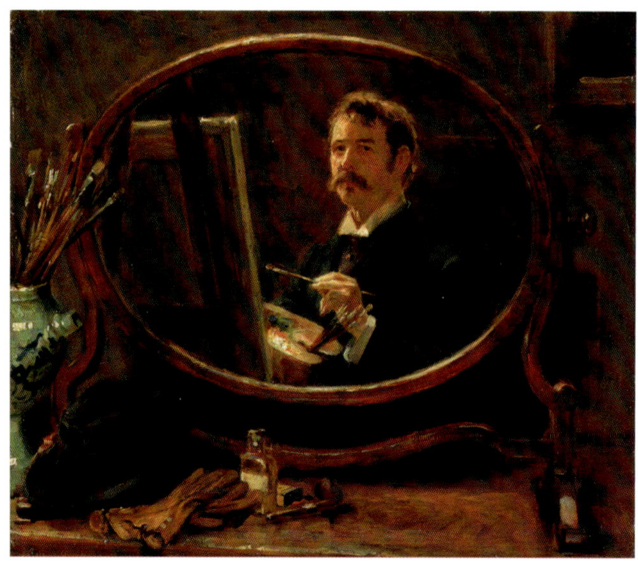

Ralph Hedley
Self-portrait, 1895
Oil on canvas, 43.2 x 50.8 cm
Given by W. Parker Brewis, 1940

In this self-portrait, Hedley has shown himself with painting equipment and fashionable gloves and hat. The picture probably commemorates his election as President of the Bewick Club in the summer of 1895. The Bewick Club was an artists' exhibiting and educational society. The picture was never exhibited in Hedley's lifetime and was given to a friend.

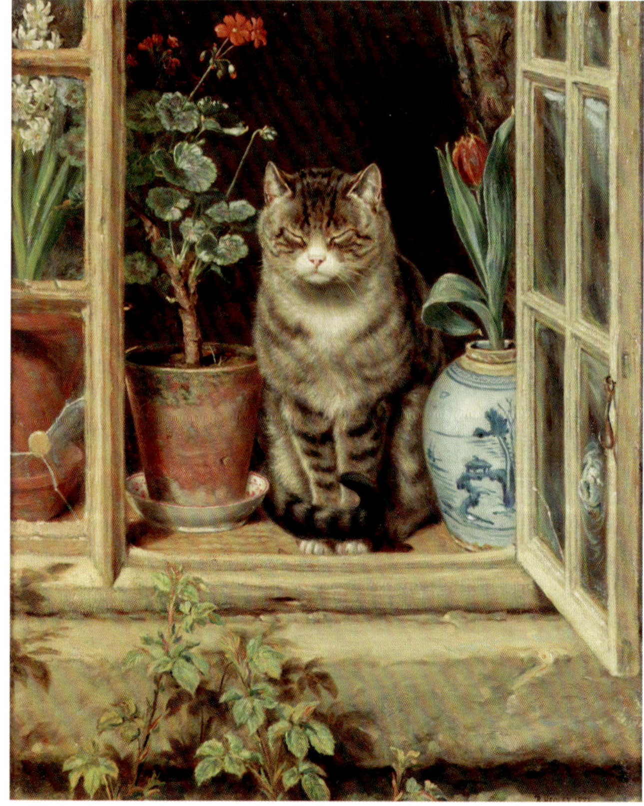

Ralph Hedley
Blinking in the Sun (Cat in a Cottage Window), 1881
Oil on canvas, 53 x 42.9 cm
Purchased 1970

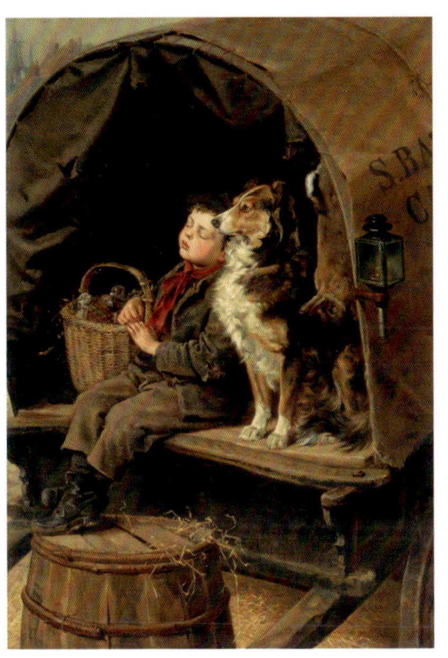

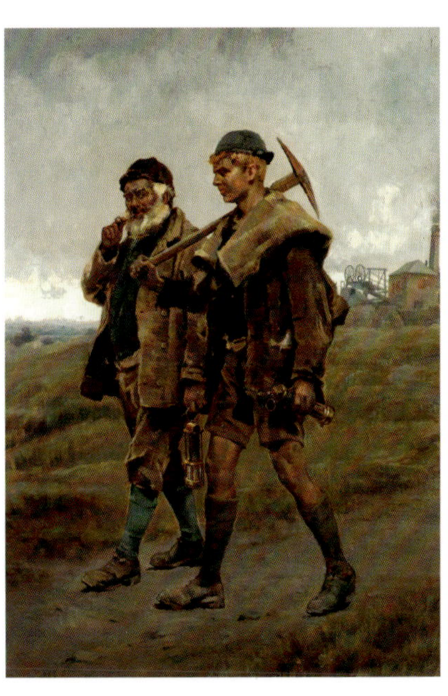

Left:
Ralph Hedley
Last in Market, 1885
Oil on canvas, 123.2 x 86.3 cm
Given by Mrs S.S. Simms, 1935

Country children often had to make long journeys to market, setting off very early. This boy has fallen asleep on the carrier's cart that will take him home at the end of the day. Hedley recorded that the picture was intended to represent the Bigg Market in Newcastle. However, he painted it in his studio (in Blackett Street, Newcastle), rather than in the market itself. The model was the brother of an apprentice in Hedley's woodcarving workshop.

Right:
Ralph Hedley
Going Home, 1888
Oil on canvas, 76.5 x 55.9 cm
Given by Miss Ellen Bicknell, 1985

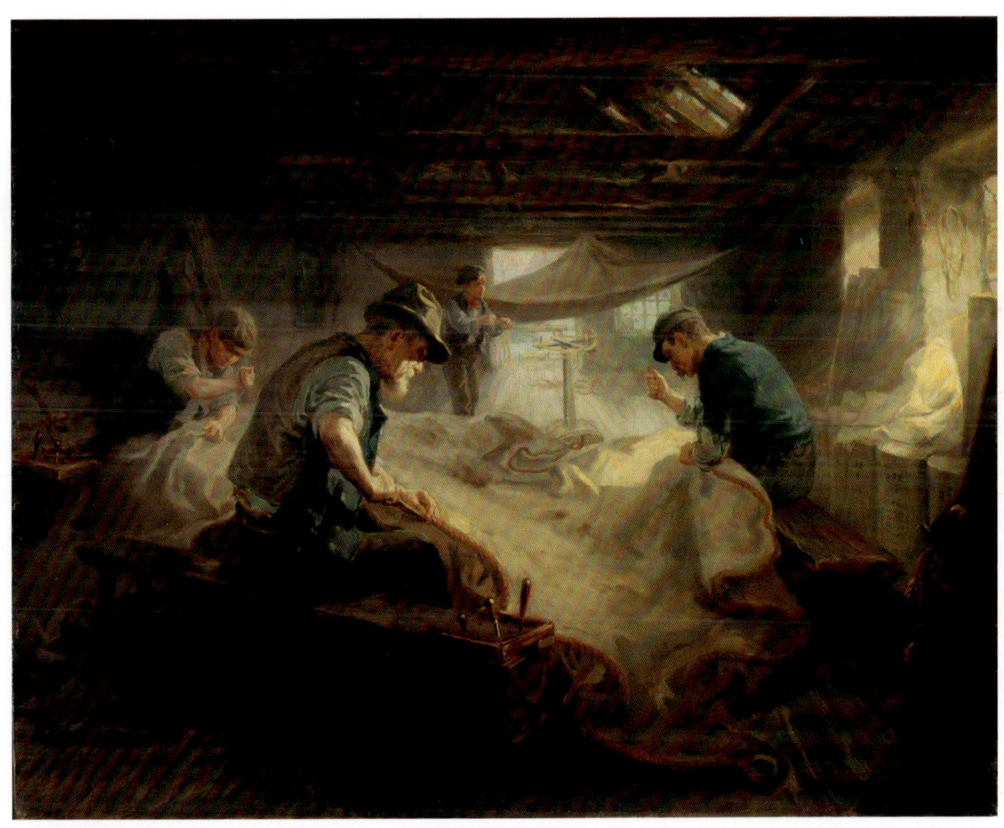

Ralph Hedley
The Sail Loft, 1908
Oil on canvas, 86.6 x 109.7 cm
Given by Miss Wilson, 1940

Daniel Maclise (1806–1870)
Alfred the Saxon King (Disguised as a Minstrel)
in the Tent of Guthrum the Dane, exhibited 1852
Oil on canvas, 122.2 x 219.4 cm
Given by Samuel Smith, JP, 1933

During the nineteenth century history painting was
considered the highest of the subjects to which
artists could aspire, together with the study of the
figure and religious art. History paintings were
intended to be morally uplifting, or to inspire the
viewer. One of the heroes of history painting was
Alfred the Great, the ninth-century philosopher
king of Wessex, who came to represent an ideal of
good government and national pride, passing from
history into legend.

Daniel Maclise chose to feature one of the
legends regarding Alfred in this large painting.
Based on a text from John Speed's *History of Great
Britain* (1611), it relates the story of when Alfred
disguised himself as a common minstrel and
entered the camp of Guthrum the Dane and his
invading army. Witnessing their negligent security
and overhearing Guthrum's battle plans, Alfred was
able to recapture Wessex from the Danes.

Alfred is shown in the centre of the painting, a
Christ-like figure wearing the clothes of a pilgrim,
surrounded by the pagan Danes, who are drinking,
gambling and fighting among themselves. Guthrum
reclines behind him inside a stage-like tent,
surrounded by his generals and the Danish ladies.
The colours within the painting are vibrant and
bright, and there is an incredible level of detail in
the figures, foliage and landscape. Maclise's style of
painting is similar to the techniques practised by
the Pre-Raphaelite artists at this time, although he
was not associated with the group.

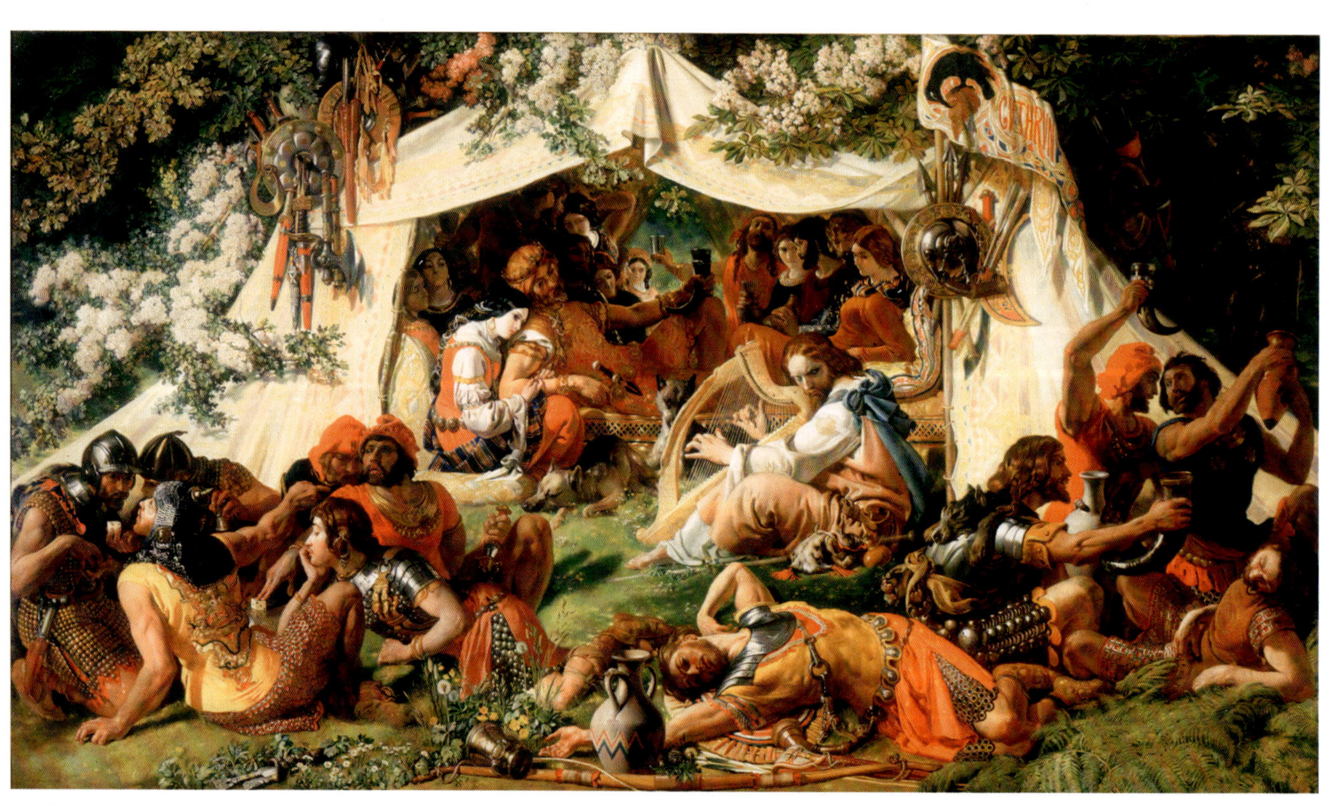

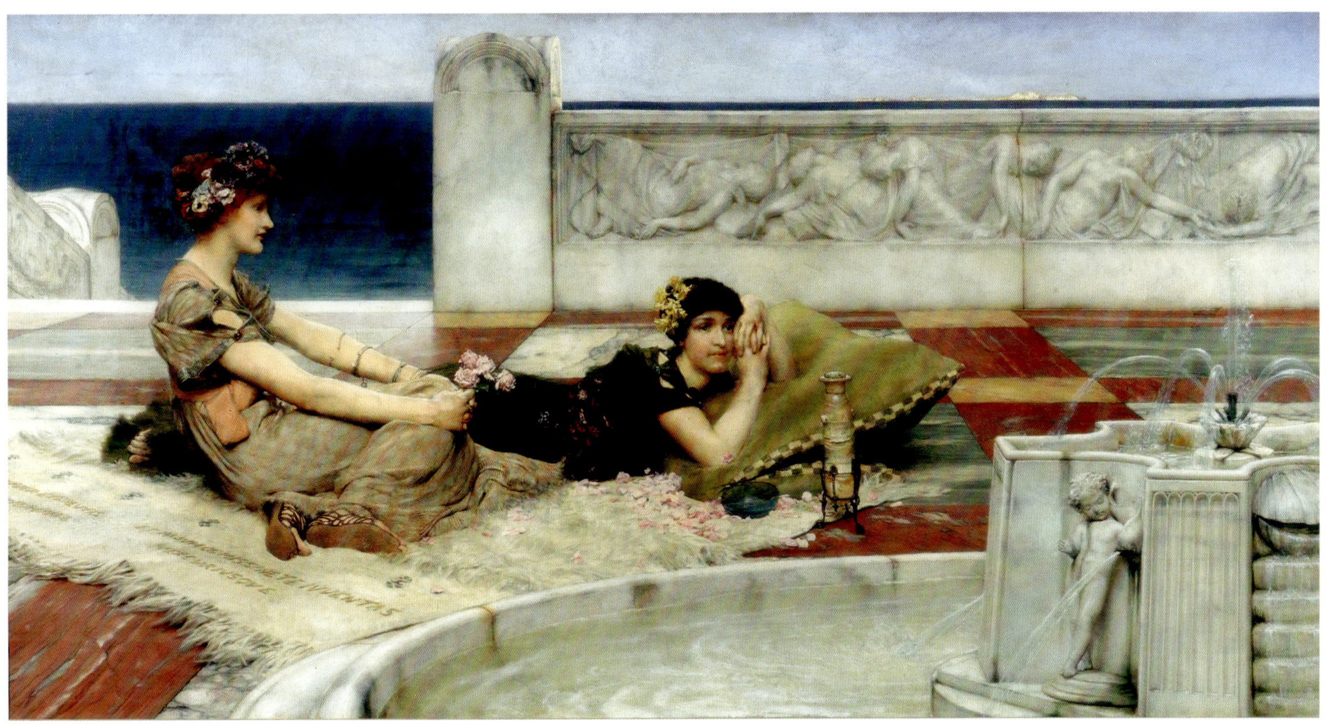

Sir Lawrence Alma-Tadema (1836–1912)
Love in Idleness (Love's Votaries),
exhibited 1891
Oil on canvas, 87 x 165.5 cm
Given by George Henderson, 1934

Sir Lawrence Alma-Tadema's paintings of beautiful young women in convincing Roman-style settings were very popular in the late nineteenth century. The realistic detail of his pictures was based on Roman wall paintings and sculpture, and he had seen Roman works of art during his honeymoon in 1863, when he and his wife visited the ruined cities of Herculaneum and Pompeii in Italy. Scenes inspired by Classical stories or themes were particularly popular with Victorian audiences, who likened the glories of the ancient Roman Empire to those of the British Empire. After Alma-Tadema moved to London from the Continent in 1870, he concentrated almost entirely on these subjects, although he also painted landscapes and portraits.

The two young women in this painting are surrounded by flowers – on their clothes, in their hair and scattered on the ground around them – reflecting their beauty. 'Love in Idleness' is an old name for the pansy flower, and as pansies also traditionally represent 'thoughts', the artist may be referring to the women's thoughts as they sit dreaming of their lovers. This theme is continued by the roses and rose petals, flowers representing romantic love, and the Latin text on the rug, which is a quotation from Horace's *Ode to Venus* (published 23 BC). The pale marble of the balustrade contrasts with the vivid azure-blue of the sea, at the top left of the painting. There is no middle ground visible; instead the foreground is abruptly juxtaposed with the distant horizon to create a dramatic effect.

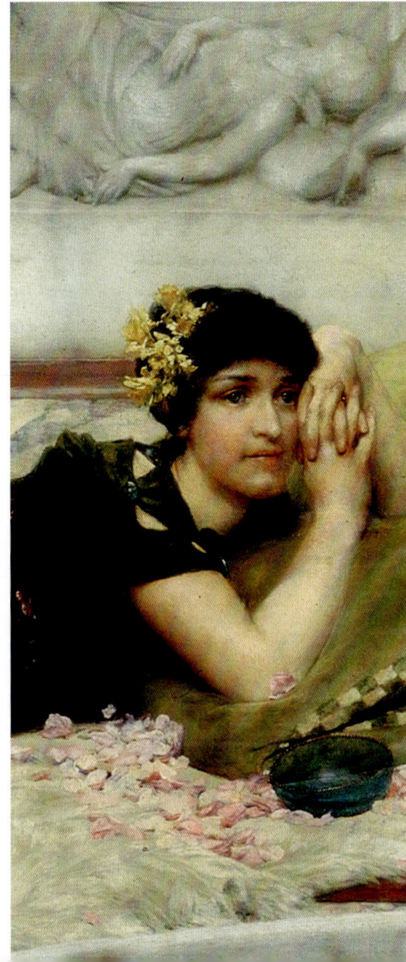

Utagawa Kunisada (1786–1864)
Evening Cool at Shijo-Kawara, 1852
Colour woodblock print (triptych), 35.7 x 75 cm
Given by A.H. Higginbottom, 1919

Shijo-Kawara is an area in central Kyoto, Japan, at the inter-section of Shijo (Fourth Street) and Kawara. Located alongside the Kamo (the main river running north–south through the city), it became a popular theatre and entertainment district during the Edo period (1615–1868). The tradition of Kabuki theatre, particular to Japanese culture, is believed to have originated from dancing and singing taking place on the dry riverbeds.

In the summer, platforms standing in the river shallows as seen in this print became sites for relaxing, drinking tea and smoking while enjoying the cooling river breeze. The seated figure central to this activity and shown on the right of this triptych is Prince Genji, hero of an eleventh-century novel. Comprising 53 chapters, Genji's romantic adventures were a popular subject for *ukiyo-e* prints (an artistic style depicting scenes of everyday life) and here he is being served and entertained by several female companions.

Like many artists working in Japan during the Edo period, Kunisada was identified by various names. This print bears the name Toyokuni, also the name of Kunisada's master. It was not until over a decade after the death of his master that Kunisada was allowed the honour of taking the name Toyokuni III. This print is part of a large collection of Japanese items, including more work by Kunisada as well as applied art, gifted to the gallery in 1919 by one collector.

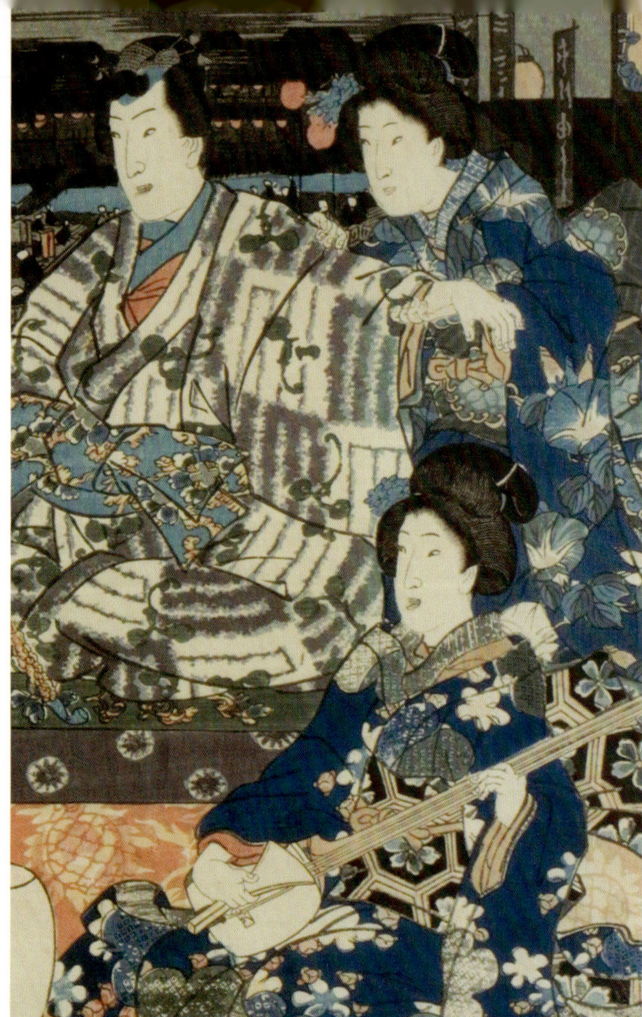

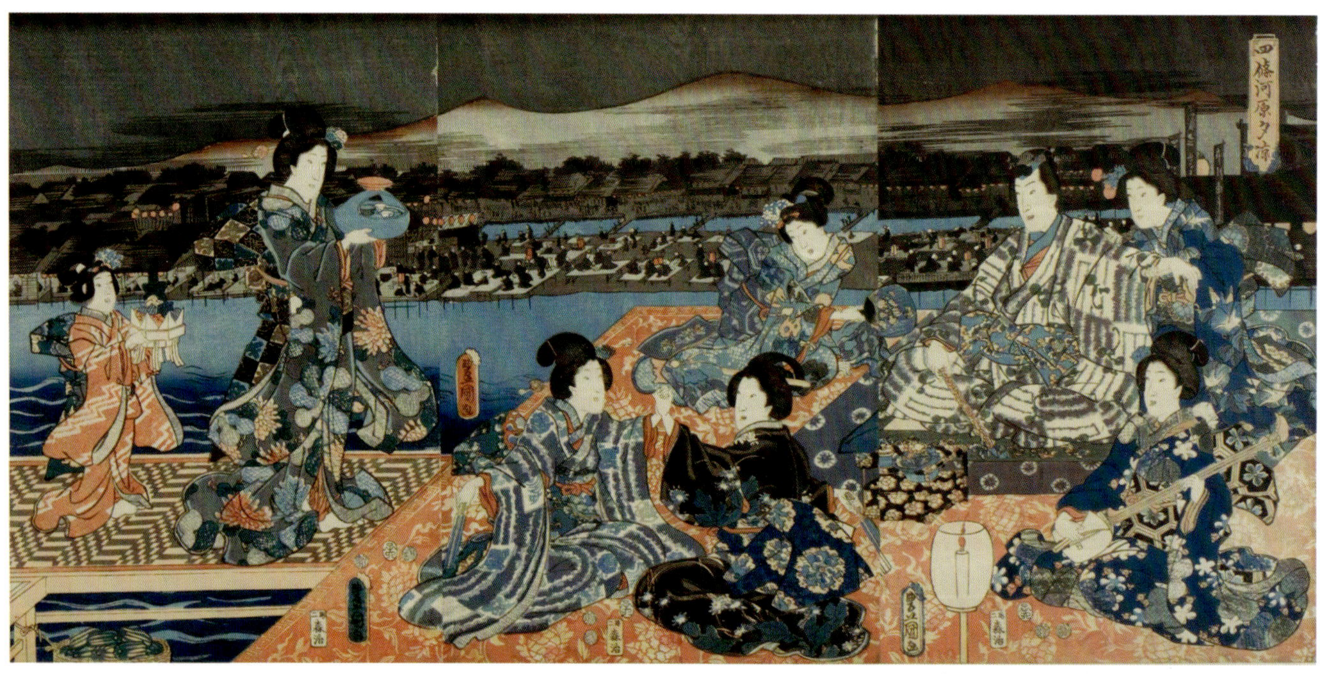

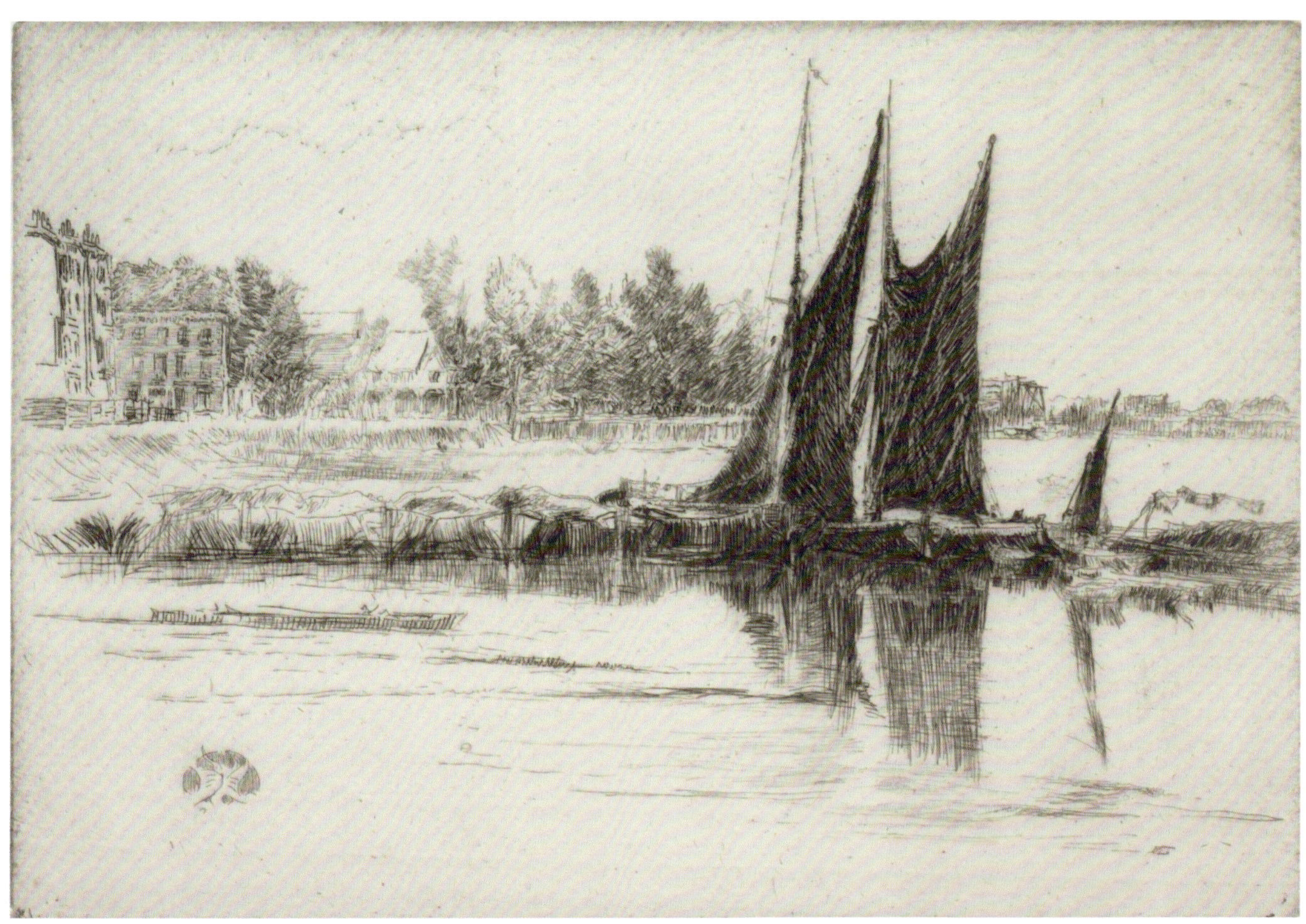

James Abbot McNeill Whistler (1834–1903)
Hurlingham, 1879
Etching, 13.9 x 20.1 cm
Given by George E. Henderson, 1934

James Abbot McNeill Whistler was an American-born, British-based artist. He worked in a wide variety of styles that included Impressionism, Symbolism and Art Nouveau, and was especially influential in the Tonalist Movement. He was a catalyst for those who wanted to break away from prescribed academic methods and is credited with being the first American modernist to influence European art. Whistler is best known for his extraordinary portraits in oils, but he was also a prolific printmaker, working in etching, lithography and drypoint. He gained a significant reputation for his skill in these processes, and took great care not only in the printing of his work, but also the selection of paper used. At the beginning and end of his career, he placed great emphasis on cleanness of line, although in a middle period he experimented more with inking and the use of plate-tone.

Hurlingham is one of several views of boats on the Thames Whistler made during the late 1870s, considered to include some of his most successful and accomplished prints. It shows a beautiful merging of Western and Japanese styles. He has signed the work using his characteristic abstract butterfly monogram, first developed during the 1860s and based on potters' marks he had seen on East Asian porcelain. However, he added a 'sting' to the tail of the butterfly, wanting it to represent not only the gentle, sensitive side of his personality, but also his quick temper and argumentative spirit. Whistler always placed this monogram very carefully, to ensure it did not disturb the overall composition of the artwork.

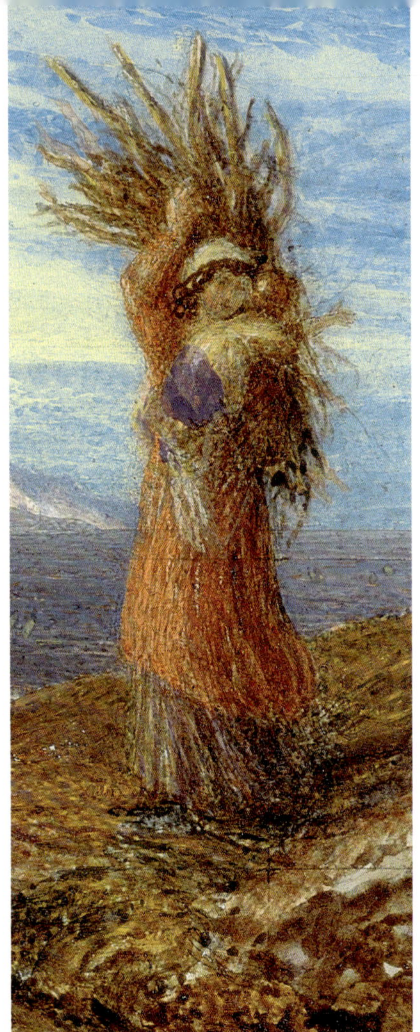

Samuel Palmer (1805–1881)
The Rising Moon, 1859
Watercolour, bodycolour and pencil on paper, 18.9 x 42.8 cm
Given by the Walker Mechanics Institute, 1942

From as early as the fourteenth century, artists have used opaque water-based paint (gouache or bodycolour) as it gives vibrant colours. Opaque water-colour paint became more popular as the nineteenth century progressed and a wider range of colours became available. There are many examples in the Laing's collection showing the stronger effects possible with this medium, as nineteenth-century scenes demonstrate the new bright colours and meticulous techniques adopted by numerous artists at this time.

Samuel Palmer became an artist at a young age, and was influenced by his friend and mentor William Blake. Palmer's early work shows an interest in the 'primitive' artists of the fifteenth and sixteenth centuries, and in the years immediately after Blake's death in 1833, he led a group of artists based at Shoreham in Kent, who called them-selves the 'Shoreham Ancients'. The group set out to create a new 'Golden Age', and Palmer in particular produced masterpieces of poetic landscape, with every element in the scene imbued with emotion: nature viewed with an intensity that imparts its own unique significance.

Palmer's romantic vision of the countryside is expressed in this important watercolour. The girl's long flowing robes suggest timelessness while her huge sheaf of corn indicates the fruitfulness of nature. The rising moon of the title illuminates the sky, while the landscape and village are bathed in the last golden light from the setting sun and thick paint creates jewel-like beads of colour. The blue sea and the style of buildings suggest that the picture was inspired by sketches that Palmer made on his long honeymoon trip to Italy in 1837–39, after which he worked mainly in watercolour.

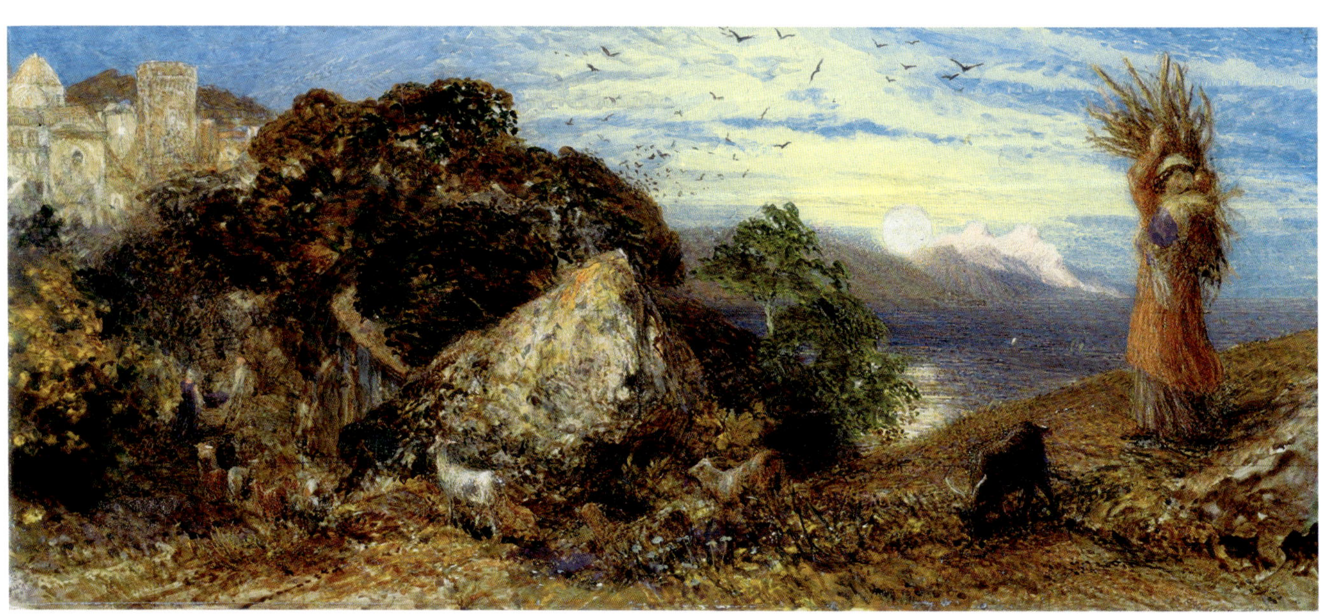

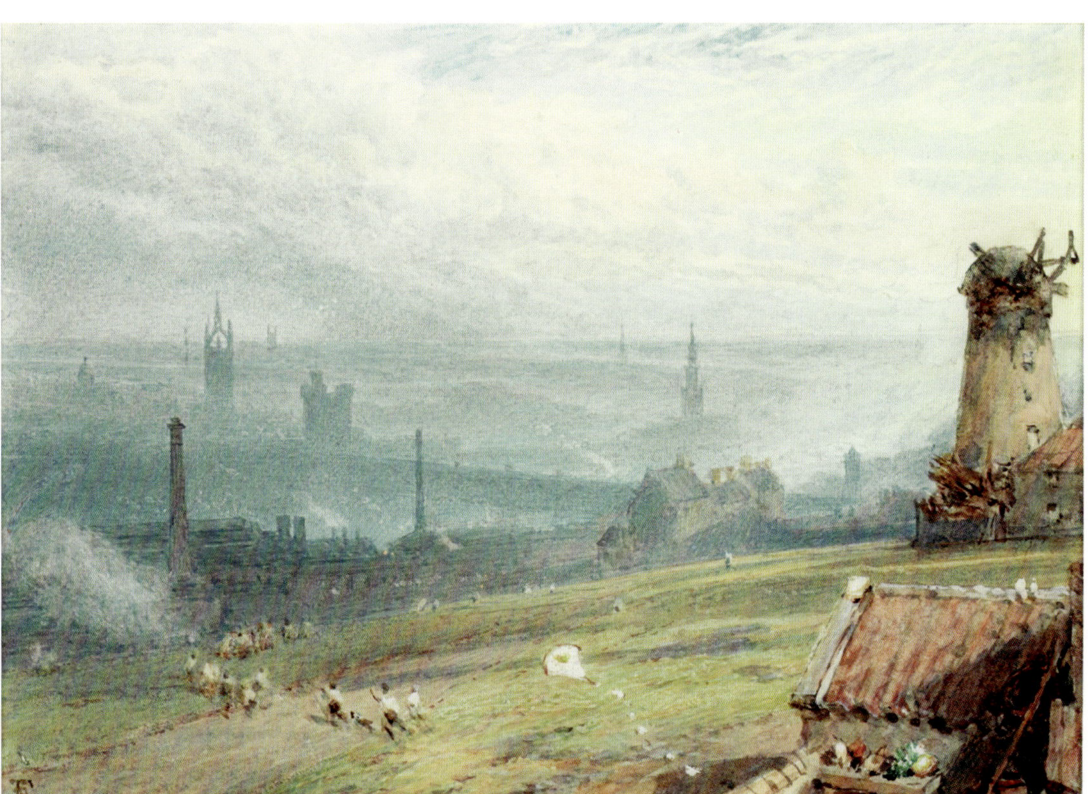

Myles Birket Foster (1825–1899)
***Newcastle upon Tyne from the Windmill Hills,
Gateshead***, *c.*1870
Watercolour and bodycolour on paper, 12.6 x 17.7 cm
Purchased 1919

Myles Birket Foster was born in North Shields, but
moved to London at an early age. Initially trained
as a wood-engraver, he found work as a book
illustrator while he taught himself to paint in
watercolours, and went on to be one of the most
successful English watercolourists of his generation.
After his death, his obituary in *The Times* referred to
him as 'certainly the most popular water-colour
artist of our time'. Birket Foster became an
Associate of the 'Old' Watercolour Society (later the
Royal Watercolour Society) in 1860, and over a
period of more than 20 years exhibited some 400
paintings at the Royal Academy. He travelled widely

throughout Europe and painted dramatic landscape scenes from Scotland to the Mediterranean,
sometimes on a very large scale. Many of the works
for which he is best known were, however, made
in Surrey, showing sentimental views of the
contemporary English countryside.

He also visited the North East and painted a
number of views of the area, such as *Newcastle
upon Tyne from the Windmill Hills, Gateshead*.
This tiny work, probably a page from a sketchbook,
appears to have been painted from the window
of one of the windmills, most of which were used
for grinding corn. Children often appear in Birket
Foster's watercolours and in this picture they are
racing down the hill with kites. The distinctive
landmarks of Newcastle's Norman castle and the
lantern tower of St Nicholas's Church emerge from
the bluish smoky haze produced by the industry of
the riverside.

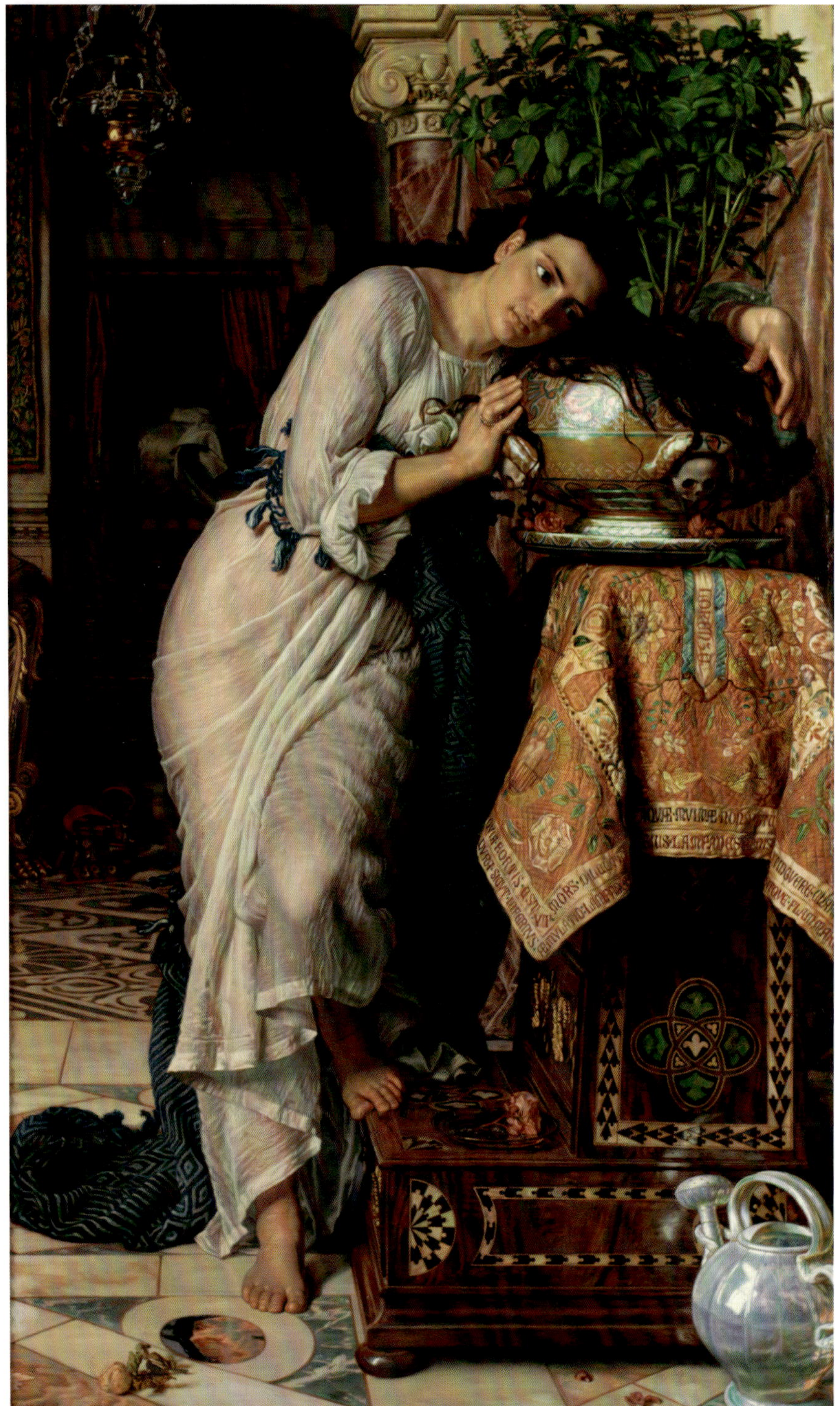

William Holman Hunt (1827–1910)
Isabella and the Pot of Basil, 1867
Oil on canvas, 187 x 116.5 cm
Given by Dr Wilfred Hall, 1953

And she forgot the stars, the moon, and sun,
And she forgot the dells where waters run,
And she forgot the chilly autumn breeze;
She had no knowledge when the day was done,
And the new moon she saw not: but in peace
Hung over her sweet Basil evermore,
And moisten'd it with tears unto the core.

(John Keats, 'Isabella; or, The Pot of Basil',
stanza LIII, 1820)

This painting illustrates a poem by the writer John Keats, published in 1820, which was based on a medieval story from Giovanni Boccaccio's *Decameron*. It tells the story of Isabella, whose lover, Lorenzo, was murdered by her cruel and disapproving brothers. Grief-stricken, she took Lorenzo's head and kept it hidden in a pot of basil. Her brothers later discovered this gruesome secret and stole the head, leaving Isabella to die of sorrow. Her mournful pose and expression, the dying roses on the ground and the skulls on the pot are reminders of Lorenzo's death and predict Isabella's own.

The picture was owned by James Hall, the Tynemouth collector who was a partner in the Newcastle shipping business of Palmer, Hall & Company. A member of the Newcastle Arts Association and a patron of the Bewick Club, Hall bought *Isabella* from the picture dealer Ernest Gambart in April 1870 for £1,550, a reduction from its asking price of £2,000. In his review of Hall's collection for *The Athenaeum*, F.G. Stephens described the painting's 'solid, rich and masculine execution, its powerful colouring, broad effect and fidelity to a peculiar phase of light' (*The Athenaeum*, 20 September 1873, p.374). In 1886 Hall loaned the picture to an exhibition of Hunt's work and the artist took the opportunity to clean and varnish it, only later telling Hall he had done so.

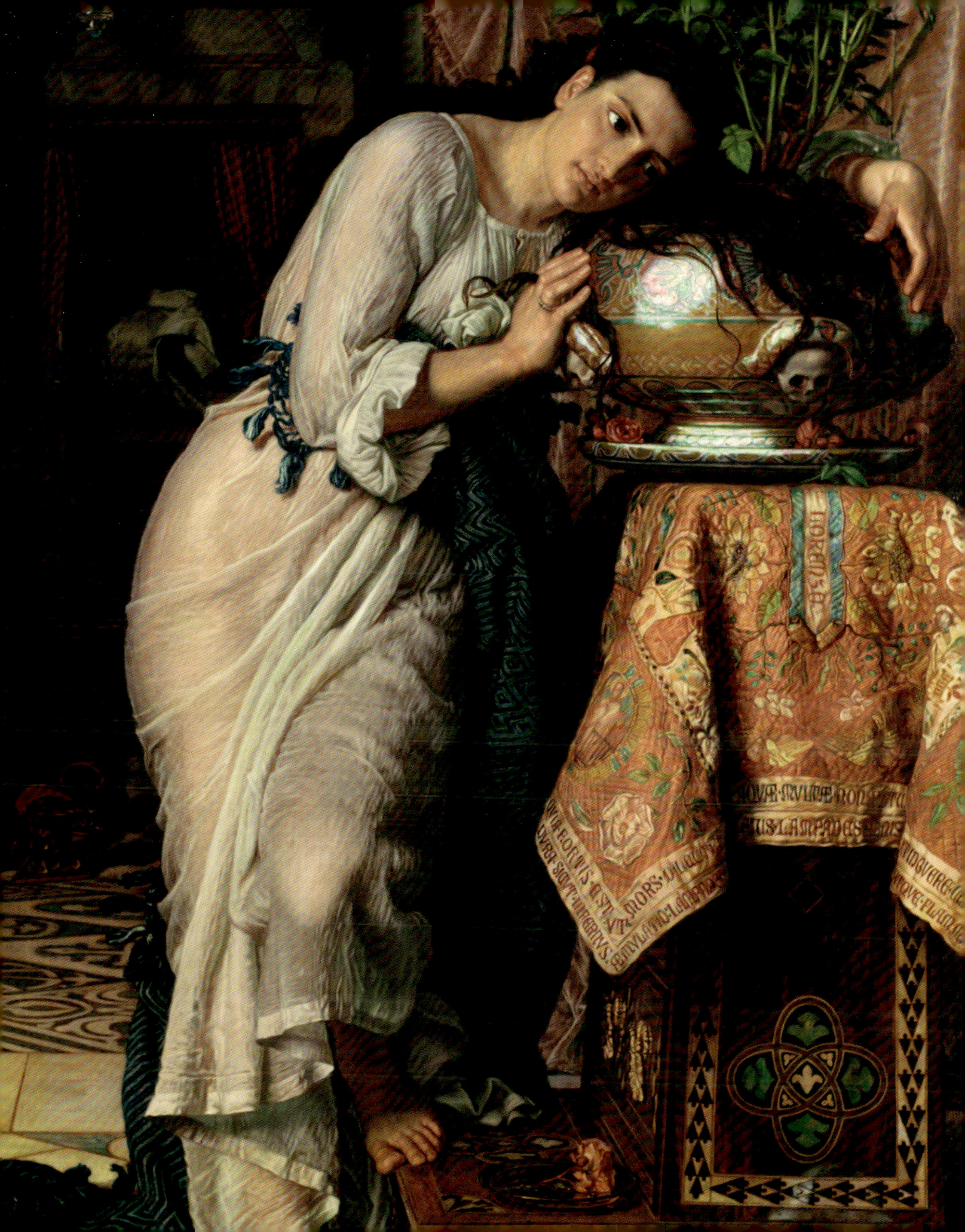
HORENSA
QVÆ·IRVIT·NON·STA
IVS·LAMPADES·SVNT
QVIA·FORTIS·EST·VT·MORS·DILECTIO
DVRA·SICVT·INFERNVS·ÆMVLATIO·LAMPADES·

The Cullercoats Colony

The small fishing village of Cullercoats on the North East coast was home to a thriving colony of artists at the end of the nineteenth century and was arguably the first British coastal colony. Cullercoats had been a popular spot for painters since the eighteenth century. However, it was not until the 1870s that artists began to live among the fisherfolk at Cullercoats. By doing so, they hoped to gain a deeper appreciation of the villagers' lives, which had changed little for hundreds of years.

The aims of the Cullercoats Colony artists were similar to those of other artists' colonies at Pont-Aven in France and Newlyn in Cornwall. However, Cullercoats has never been as famous because the artists did not often show their work outside the North East. Many of the region's finest artists worked at the Colony, while international artists such as the American painter Winslow Homer also paid long visits. It was sustained by a thriving local art market, which the Colonists themselves had largely stimulated by creating a network of art clubs, exhibition venues and sales outlets throughout the area. The number of Colony artists gradually declined over the years as artistic tastes changed and they sought more modern subjects, but important pictures continued to be produced at Cullercoats into the 1920s.

John Charlton (1849–1917)
The Women, exhibited 1910
Oil on canvas, 152.2 x 244.3 cm
Bequeathed by the artist, 1918

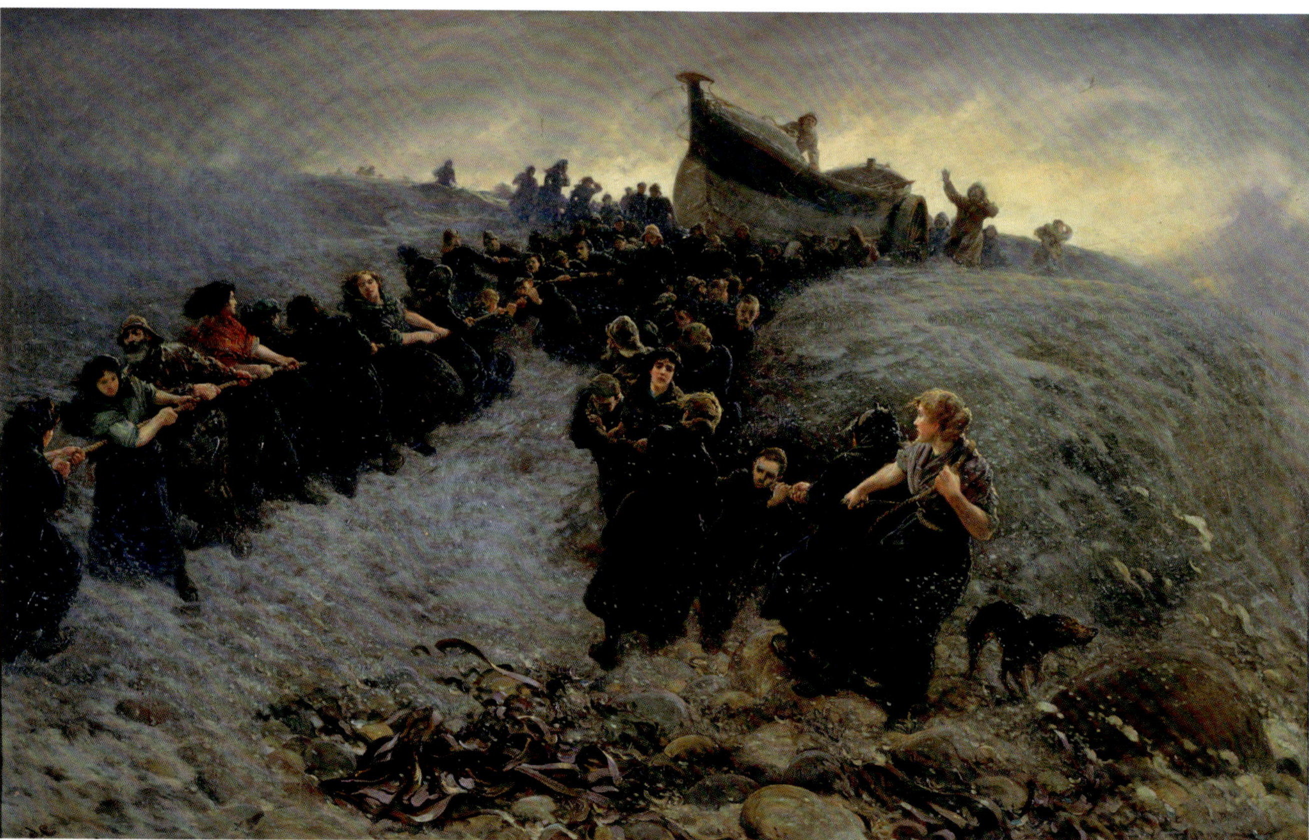

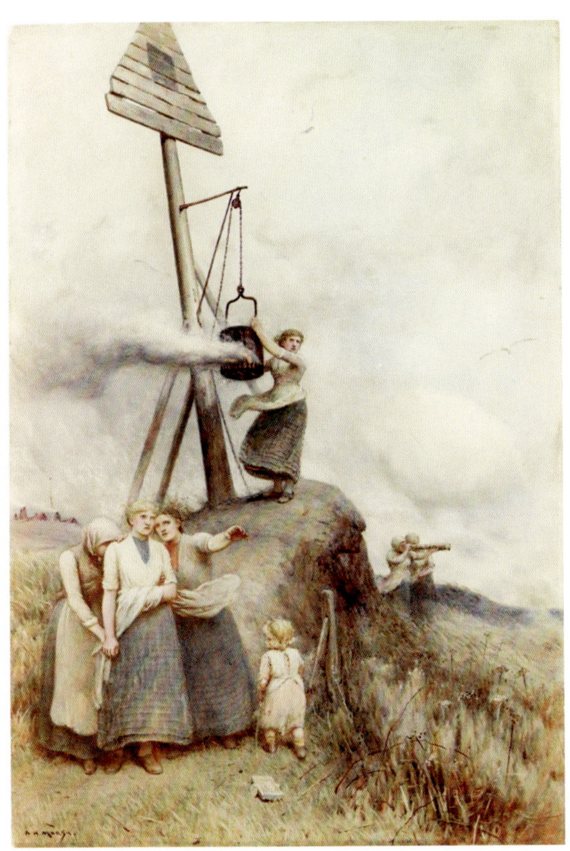

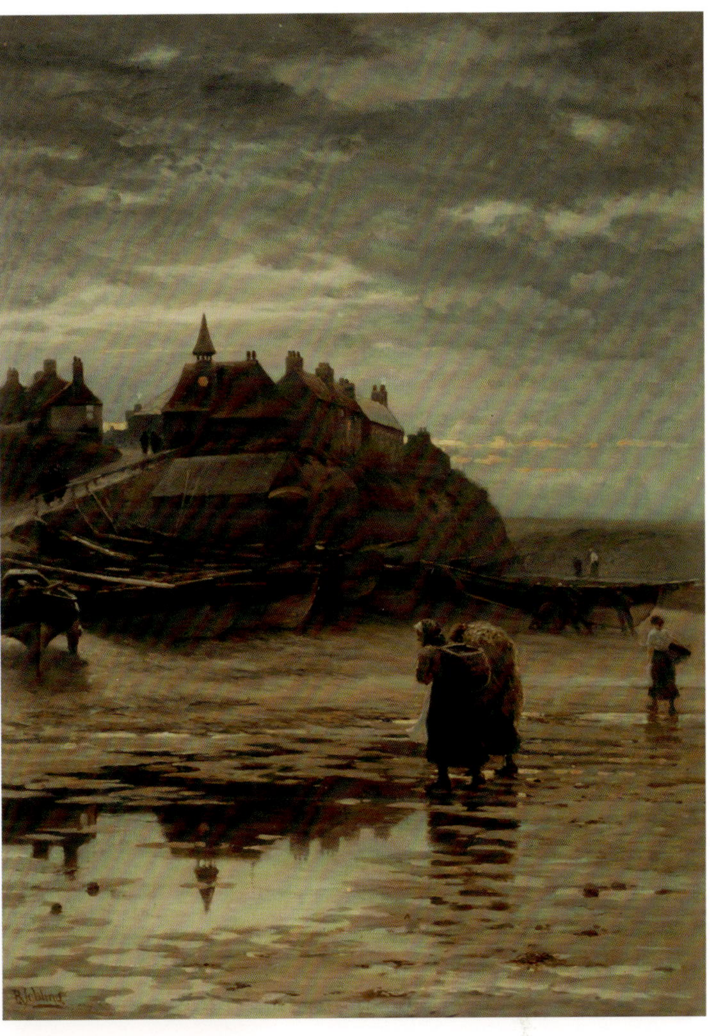

Above:
Arthur Hardwick Marsh (1842–1909)
Lighting the Beacon (Men must Work and Women must Weep), exhibited 1887
Watercolour, bodycolour and pencil on board, 78.4 x 54.1 cm
Given by J.B. Garland, 1927

Above:
Robert Jobling (1841–1923)
Darkness Falls from the Wings of Night, 1886
Oil on canvas, 128.1 x 92.2
Given by Mrs R. Robson, 1931

Left:
Henry Hetherington Emmerson (1831–1895)
A Foreign Invasion, exhibited 1871
Oil on canvas, 117.7 x 172.7 cm
Given by the City of Newcastle upon Tyne
(Parks and Cemeteries), 1972

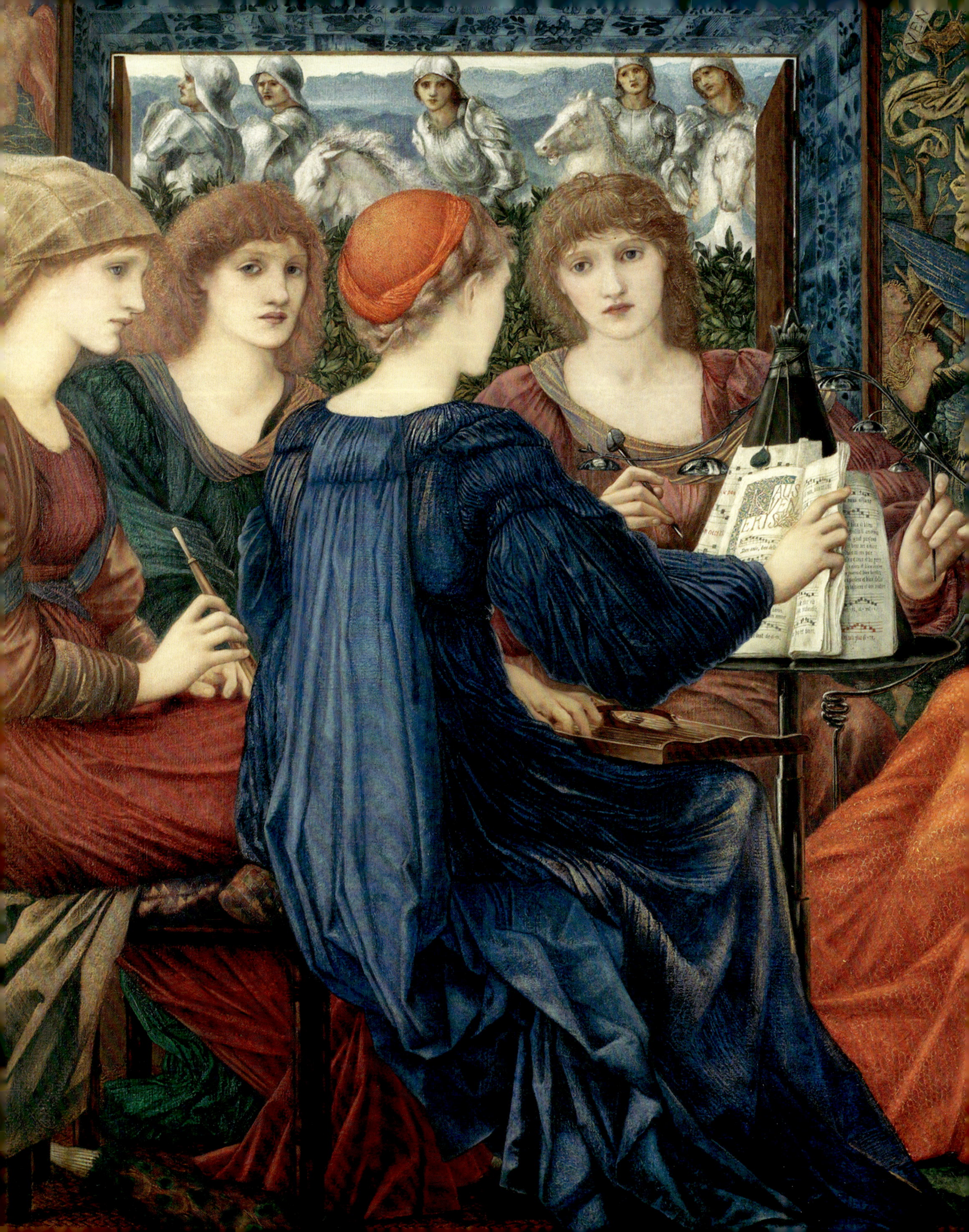

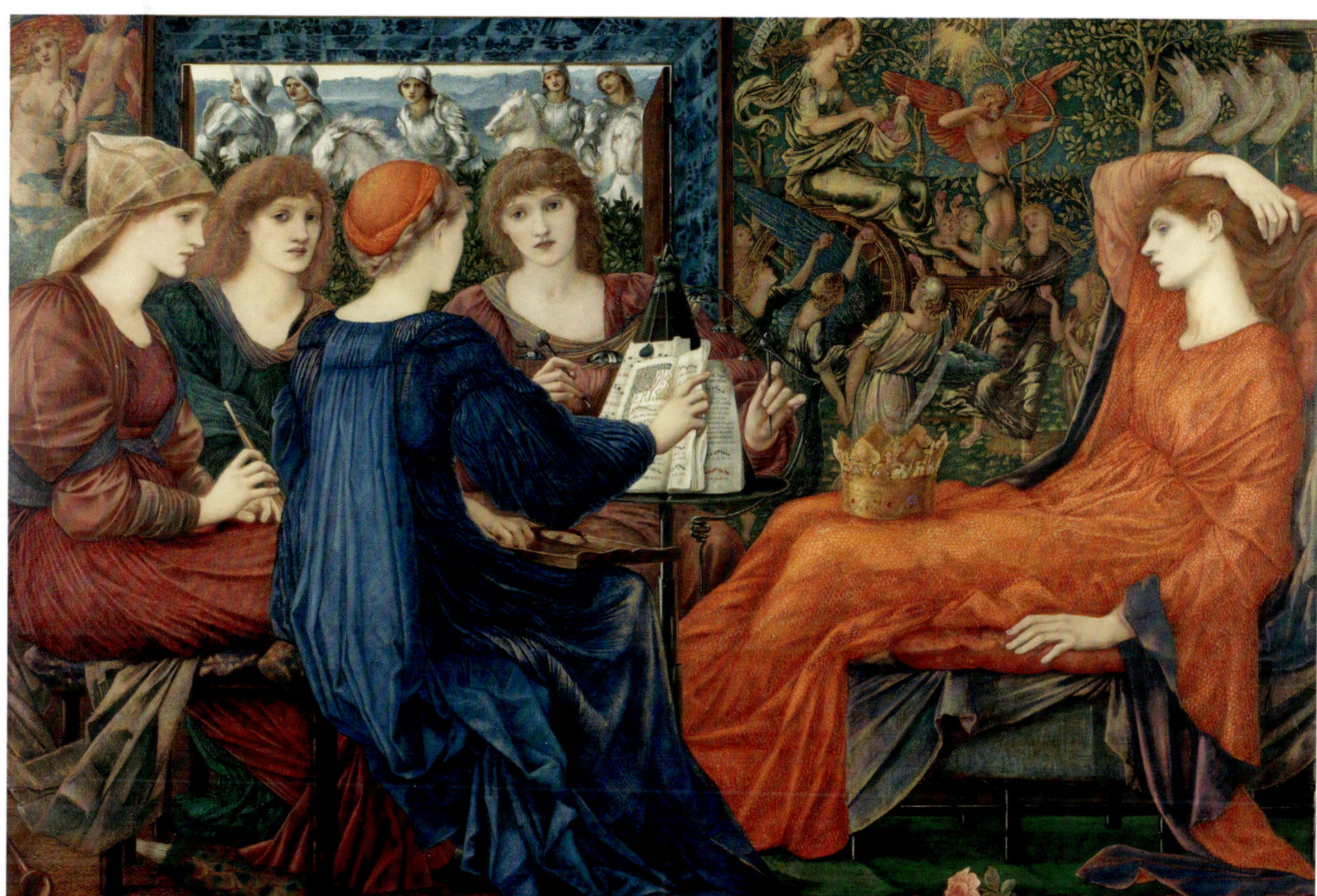

Sir Edward Coley Burne-Jones (1833–1898)
Laus Veneris, 1873–75
Oil on canvas, 122.5 x 183.3 cm
Purchased with grant aid from the Victoria and Albert Museum Purchase Grant Fund, The Art Fund, Pilgrim Trust, Friends of the Laing Art Gallery and Trustees of the John Wigham Richardson Bequest, 1972

The Laing Art Gallery collections feature outstanding paintings by important members of the Pre-Raphaelite Brotherhood. Formed in 1848 by a group of young artists and writers led by William Holman Hunt, John Everett Millais and Dante Gabriel Rossetti, the Brotherhood rejected the Victorian obsession with Raphael and the painters of the Italian Renaissance, instead admiring the simplicity and sincerity of Italian art before this time. Concentrating on medieval and poetic themes, or moral subjects set in their own times, Pre-Raphaelite paintings are characterised by the use of bright, luminous colour and close observation of nature.

Sir Edward Coley Burne-Jones was the leader of the second phase of the Pre-Raphaelite Movement and was one of the most influential painters in Britain at this time. *Laus Veneris* (meaning 'in praise of Venus') is based on the medieval legend of Tannhäuser, later the subject of an opera by Richard Wagner, and shows the legendary court of Venusberg (city of love). The knight seen in the centre of the window is Tannhäuser, who is riding off to seek forgiveness from the Pope for having given himself up to a life of pleasure in the city. The Queen's women are playing music (the food of love), while a rose, also a symbol of love, lies on the ground by the Queen. The tapestries in the background show scenes from the life of Venus (goddess of love): her birth from the sea-foam, and riding in her chariot drawn by doves with her son Cupid.

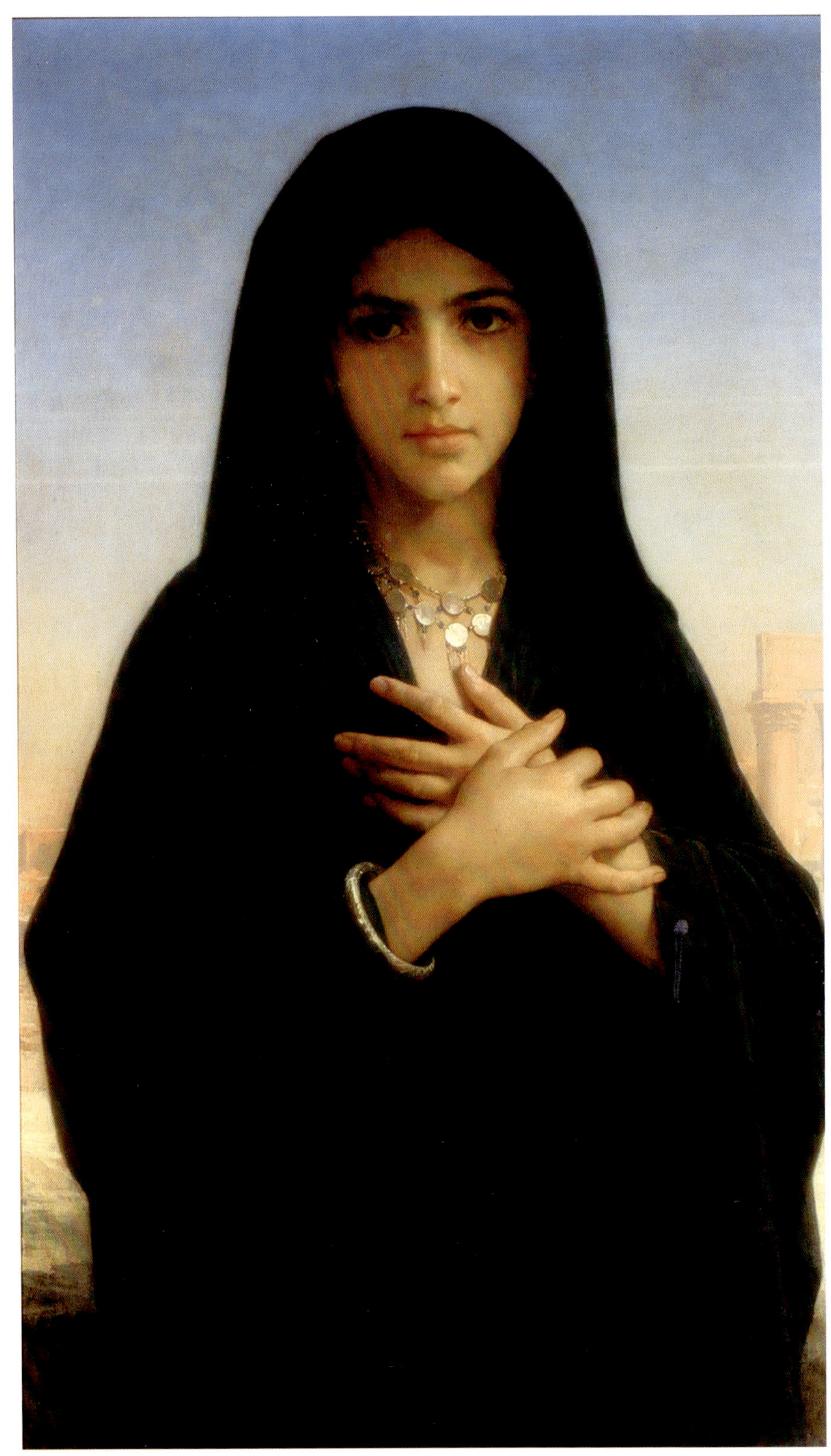

William Adolphe Bouguereau (1825–1905)
The Penitent, 1876
Oil on canvas, 88.7 x 55.5 cm
Given by Colin D. Currie, 1953

William Bouguereau was a highly successful nineteenth-century French academic painter, who worked in a very traditional style. His genre paintings and mythological subjects were modern interpretations of Classical subjects, both pagan and Christian, with an emphasis on graceful female portraits. His work was typical of the style favoured by the Paris Salon at this time and he exhibited his paintings at its annual exhibitions throughout his career. Bouguereau's work fell out of favour in the early twentieth century, as public tastes changed and more avant-garde styles became popular.

The Penitent is typical of Bouguereau's style of portrait painting: an alluring image with a smooth, highly finished surface. It is probably meant to suggest the Biblical character of Mary Magdalene, a follower of Jesus, who was the best-known penitent woman for Victorian viewers. Gold jewellery symbolises her former life of worldly pleasure, while her black robes show the religious way of life she has since taken up. The landscape behind her is hazy, suggesting heat, and Classical buildings are visible. This may refer to the notion that she spent her last days in the Greek city of Ephesus, or to the legend that confuses her with St Mary of Egypt, who was a hermit in the desert.

Sir George Clausen (1852–1944)
The Stone Pickers, 1887
Oil on canvas, 107.6 x 79.2 cm
Purchased 1907
© Clausen Estate

George Clausen began painting the rural field workers around his Hertfordshire home during the 1880s. He was influenced by the style of Rustic Naturalism employed by French painters such as Jules Bastien Lepage and Jean François Millet. This style showed the harsh realities of rural life, unlike the idyllic, gentle countryside scenes depicted by earlier artists. Such unromanticised scenes of country life were often rejected by the selectors of the Royal Academy annual exhibitions.

In pre-industrial times workers, often women and children, were employed to pick up stones from the fields so they could be ploughed and sown more easily, without damaging the metal blades of the ploughs. It was back-breaking and poorly-paid work, as can be seen in the expression of weariness in the face and posture of the young girl. Clausen has come in very close to this figure, emphasising her importance as an individual rather than just as an anonymous worker. She stands in a barren landscape, emptying stones from her rough sackcloth apron in a pile at her feet. Behind her another worker bends to her task; her face is hidden but she appears to be much older, and the viewer wonders if this symbolises the fate of the young girl, trapped in a harsh existence. Clausen has applied the paint using square-edged brushstrokes, which break down sharp lines and merge the figure with the landscape. The muted light green and brown colours also emphasise the unity of the workers and their environment.

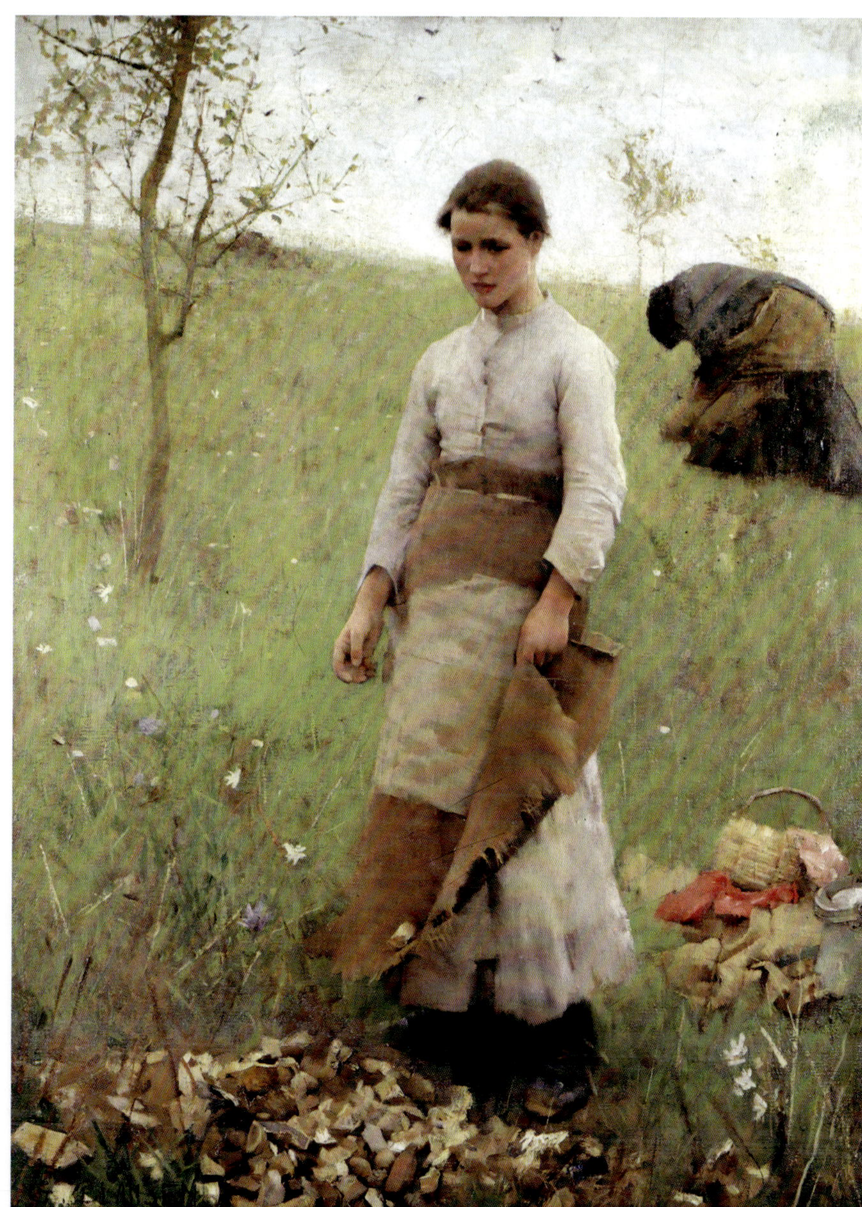

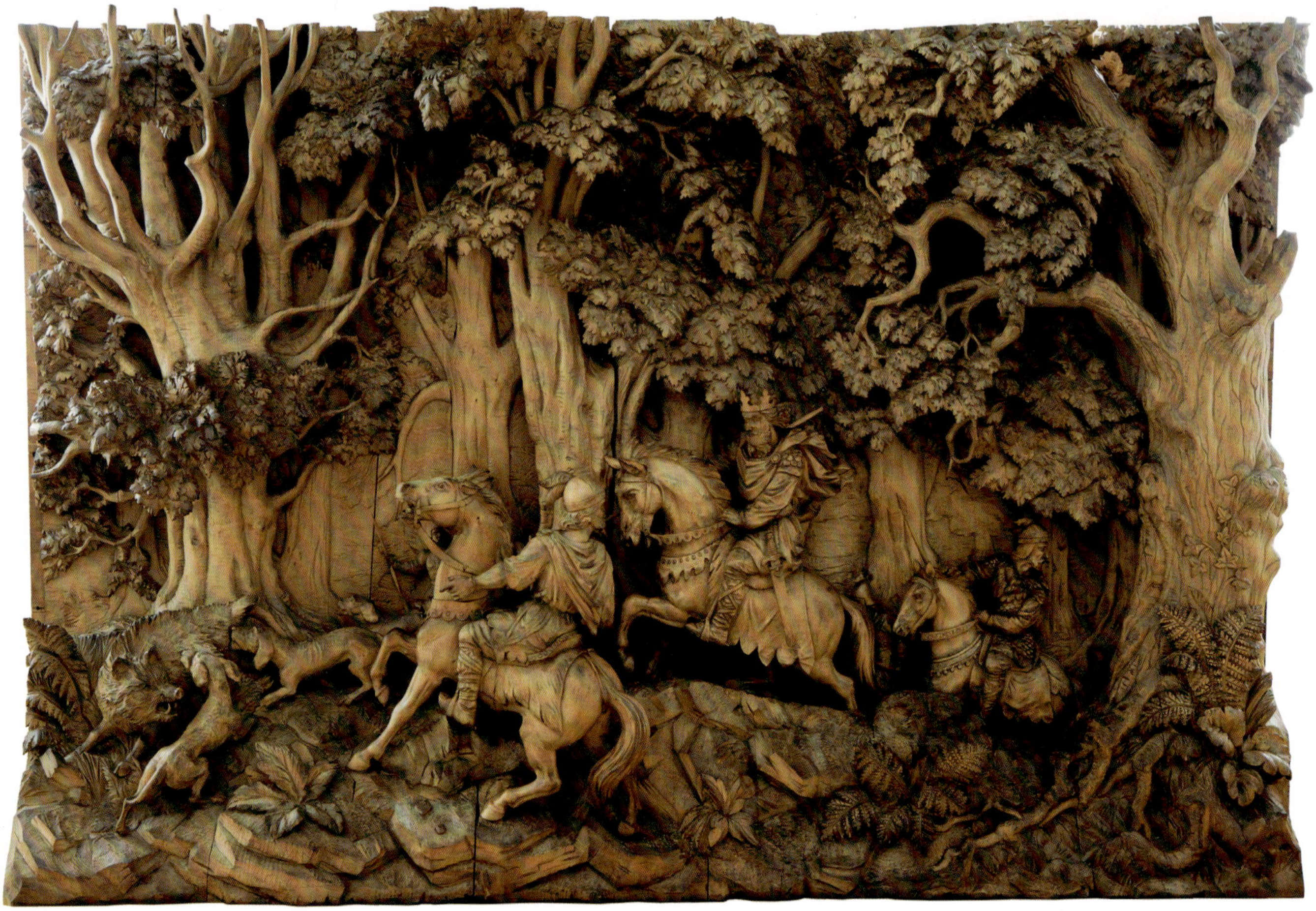

Gerrard Robinson (1834–1891)
The Boar Hunt (King Alfred in the Herdsman's Hunt), *c.*1879
Lime wood, 115 x 182 x 31 cm
Acquired 1993

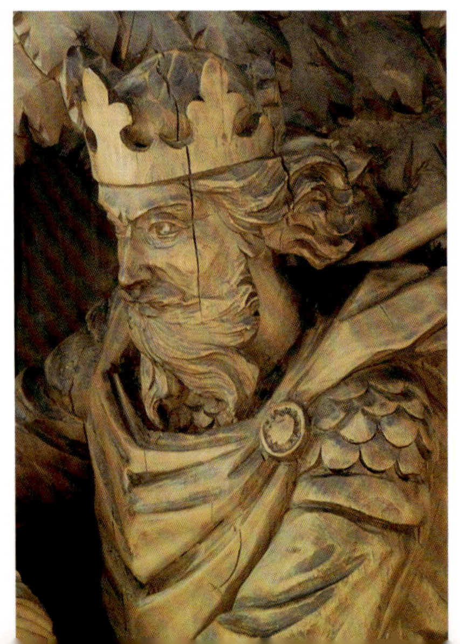

Gerrard Robinson was the most outstanding woodcarver in Northumbria during the nineteenth century, with an international reputation. The son of a blacksmith, he showed an early talent for drawing and studied at the Newcastle School of Design under William Bell Scott. His passion for woodcarving grew during his apprenticeship with Thomas Tweedy, a Newcastle carver and gilder. Robinson spent seven years as foreman of Tweedy's workshop, before setting up his own business in London.

This impressive carving shows the ninth-century King Alfred hunting wild boar in a forest. It is an 'overmantle', designed to hang above a fireplace. It has been carved in one piece from a single large block of wood, made by fitting several smaller blocks together rather than the figures being carved separately then added into the background. King Alfred achieved heroic status in the nineteenth century. He was known as 'the Great' for his wise rule of the southern part of England, defending it against Viking attack. He created a new code of law as well as fostering a revival of religion and learning.

Robinson's carvings became very famous in London. In 1866 he returned to Newcastle and was commissioned by William Wailes to produce a large amount of carved work for Saltwell Towers, Gateshead. In 1867 he was made a Freeman of the City in recognition of his talent. However, woodcarving was becoming less fashionable and his business eventually collapsed. Left in poverty, Robinson worked mainly at teaching and book illustration until his death in 1891.

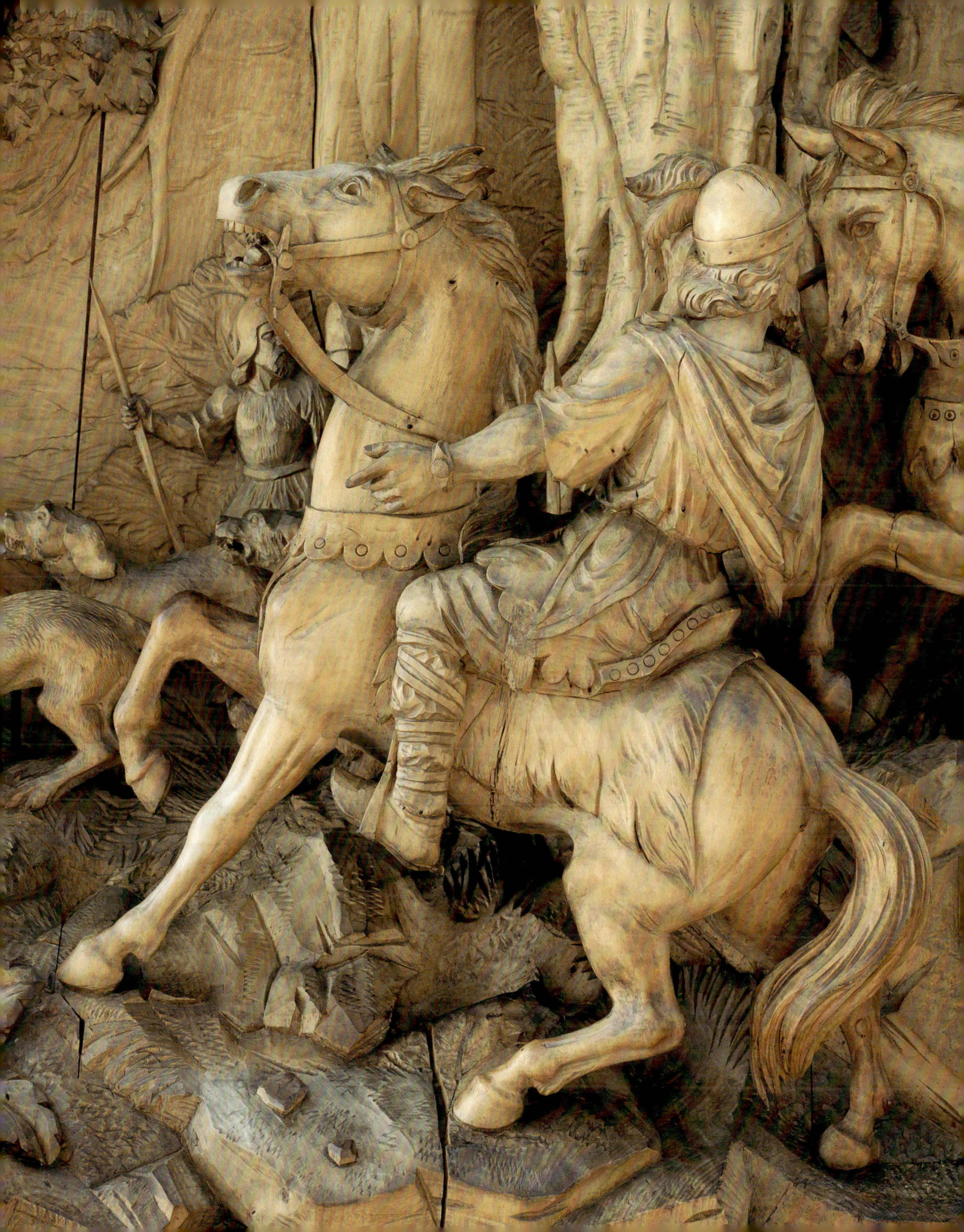

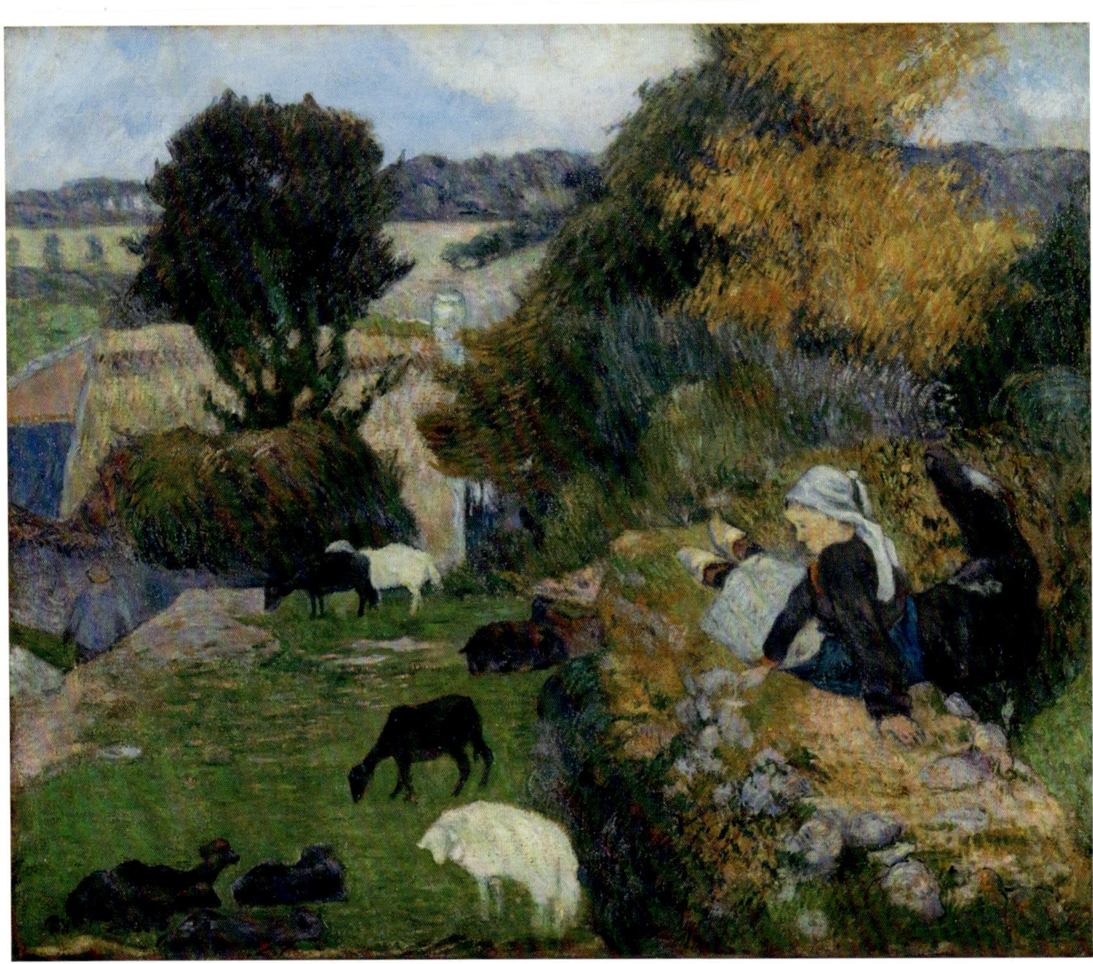

Paul Gauguin (1848–1903)
The Breton Shepherdess, 1886
Oil on canvas, 60.4 x 73.3 cm
Given by The Art Fund, 1945

This important landscape was one of the first
pictures that the French artist Paul Gauguin painted
in Pont Aven, on the coast of Brittany. The small
village attracted artists due to the picturesque
dress and folk customs of the Breton people.
Gauguin felt drawn to the harsh landscape and
Breton way of life, unspoiled by civilisation.
One of the whitewashed and thatched houses of
the village can be seen through the trees in the
background.

The Breton Shepherdess shows a young girl in
traditional Breton costume, with a white cap and
clogs. She is reclining on a wall built from stones
gathered from the steep, rocky field, watching the
sheep in the field below her. Produced at a turning
point in Gauguin's work, some areas of the picture
are painted in the Impressionist-influenced dabs of
colour he used early in his career, especially the
mosaic of blue, purple, emerald, bright green and
pink that builds up the stone wall and the grass
growing on it. Gauguin declared to his friend Henri
Delavallée that he used only pure colour, blending
it as little as possible. In contrast, the shepherdess
and the animals have been painted in a flatter, more
pattern-like manner, characteristic of the Post-
Impressionist style Gauguin developed later.
The forms of the girl and the cow beside her are
emphasised with blue outlines, and their shapes
almost merge together, which Gauguin perhaps
intended to represent the connection of the Breton
people to the ancient landscape and the lives of
the animals they tended.

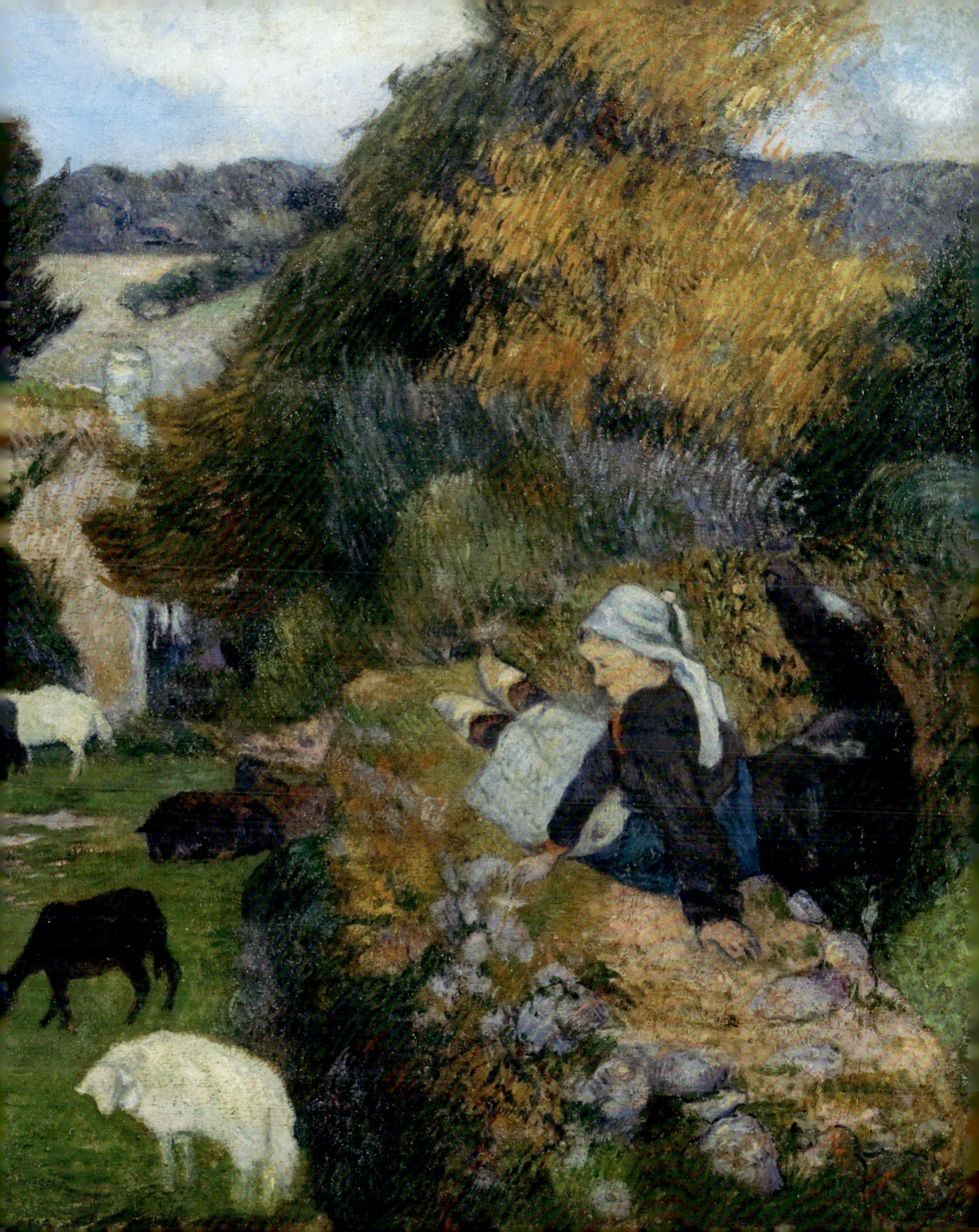

Waldo Thomas Story (1855–1915)
Fallen Angel, 1889
Marble, 93 x 183.8 x 61 cm
Given by George Collins, 1930

Born in Rome, the son of American sculptor and writer William Wetmore Story, Waldo Story followed in his father's footsteps. He inherited his father's studio in Rome, but lived and worked in Britain for most of his career. A member of the Society of British Artists, he exhibited at the Royal Academy from 1882 and also at the Grosvenor Gallery in London. During the 1880s Story became influenced by the Gothic architecture and medieval legends that fascinated his contemporaries, the Pre-Raphaelite painters. Like them, the group of Victorian British sculptors to which Story belonged were pioneering in many ways. They made freestanding, imaginative, non-commissioned sculptures for which they hoped to find buyers, rather than working to a set brief. This gave them much more artistic freedom and is one reason why sculptures such as this are so striking.

Story carved his first version of *Fallen Angel* in 1887. It was such a success that two years later he made this one, while he was living in Rome. Combining high Victorian sentiment, exquisite workmanship, naturalism and the use of exotic materials, this amazing piece, representing a guardian angel watched over sadly by a young man, demonstrates an artistic peak. Its delicacy and purity look to the Italian Renaissance and the work of artists such as Michelangelo and Donatello. Story's technique is highly accomplished, accurately re-creating surface textures through fine modelling. The white marble is evocative of human flesh, particularly in its texture, with a fine surface grain and softness, and in the way that it reflects light.

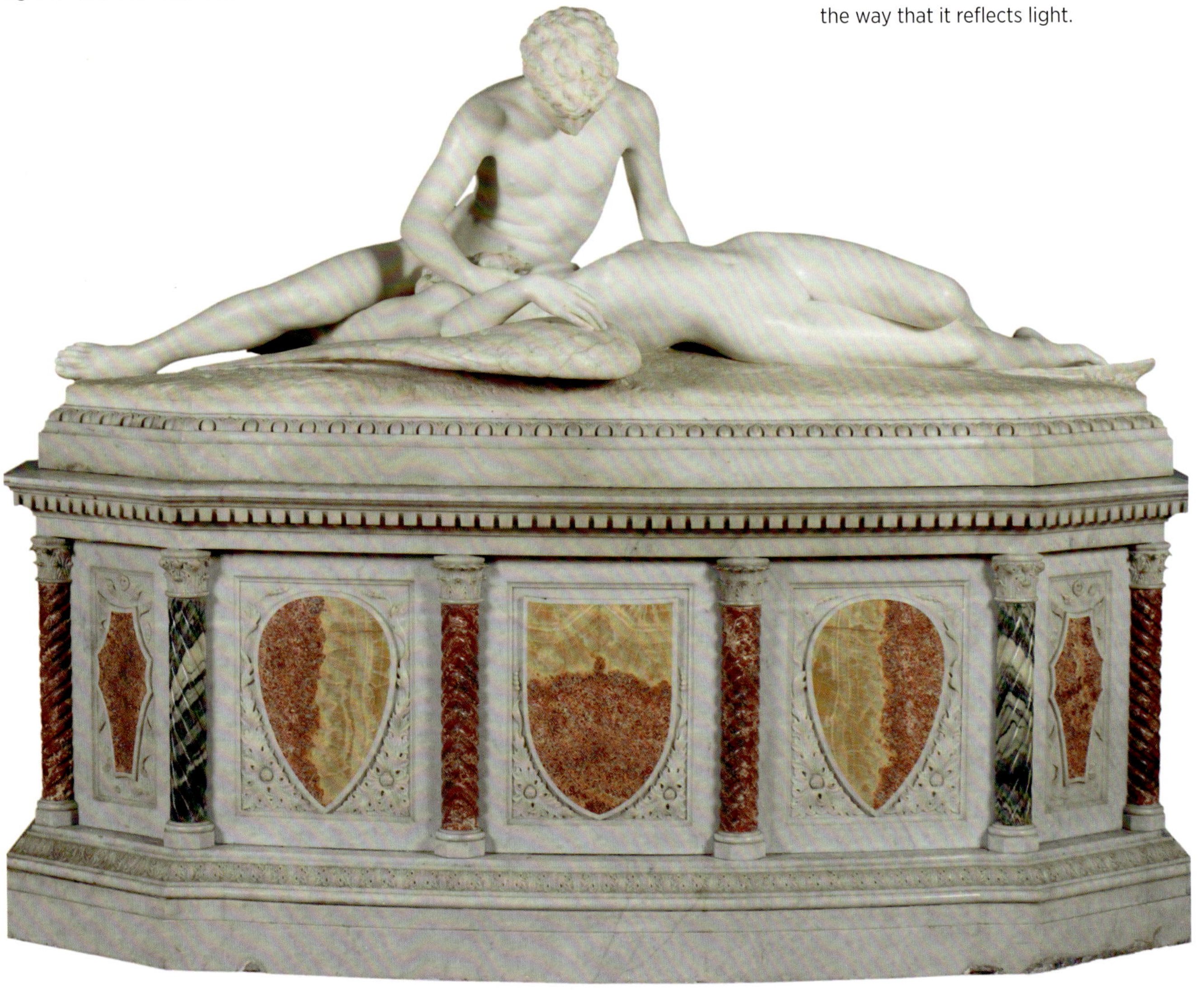

Albert Toft (1862–1949)
The Spirit of Contemplation, 1901
Bronze, 97 x 101 x 55.9 cm
Purchased 1915

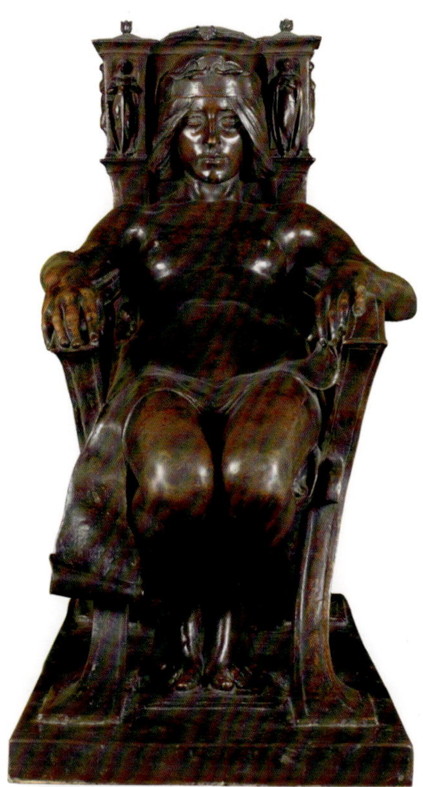

Albert Toft was born in Birmingham in 1862. His father, Charles Toft, was Chief Figure Modeller at Wedgwood from 1877 to 1888. Toft initially trained as a potter, studying at Hanley and Newcastle-under-Lyme art schools. He showed great promise and won a scholarship to the Royal College of Art at the age of 17. Toft was inspired by the Classical sculpture of ancient Greece and Rome. He studied under Italian sculptor Professor Edouard Lanteri and exhibited widely from 1885, regularly showing his work at the Royal Academy for over 60 years. Toft specialised in figurative sculpture and from his London studio produced a large number of public monuments and memorials, many of which still survive in British cities today.

The Spirit of Contemplation is an outstanding example of one of Toft's specialities: a Symbolist sculpture of an allegorical female figure. The elegant curving lines and melancholy air are features present in many works of art in the first years of the twentieth century. Blending Art Nouveau style with traditional historical, mythological and romantic subject matter, this idealised figure is shown in a dream-like state of reverie. The figure of Contemplation reclines against a chair back decorated with small figures representing Courage, Philosophy, Life and Love, suggesting that these abstractions are perhaps among those she is considering as she meditates. Toft exhibited a plaster version of this sculpture, but without the drapery over the legs, at the 1901 Royal Academy exhibition, just before the bronze was cast.

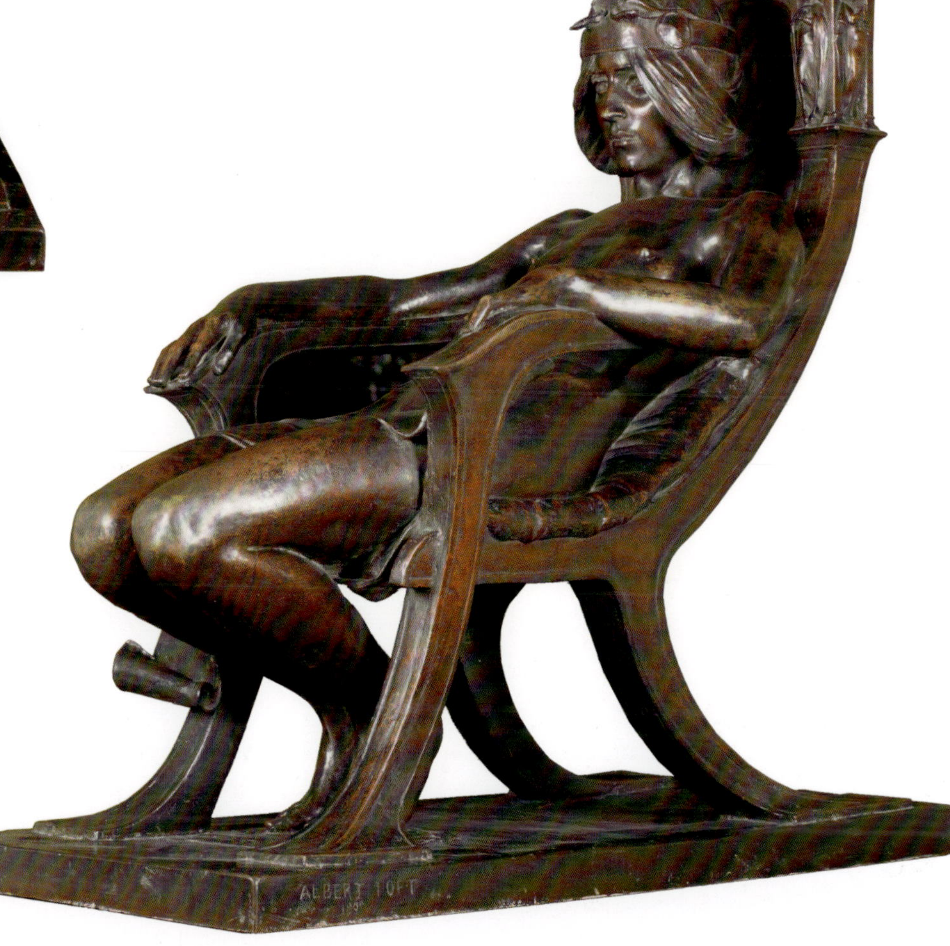

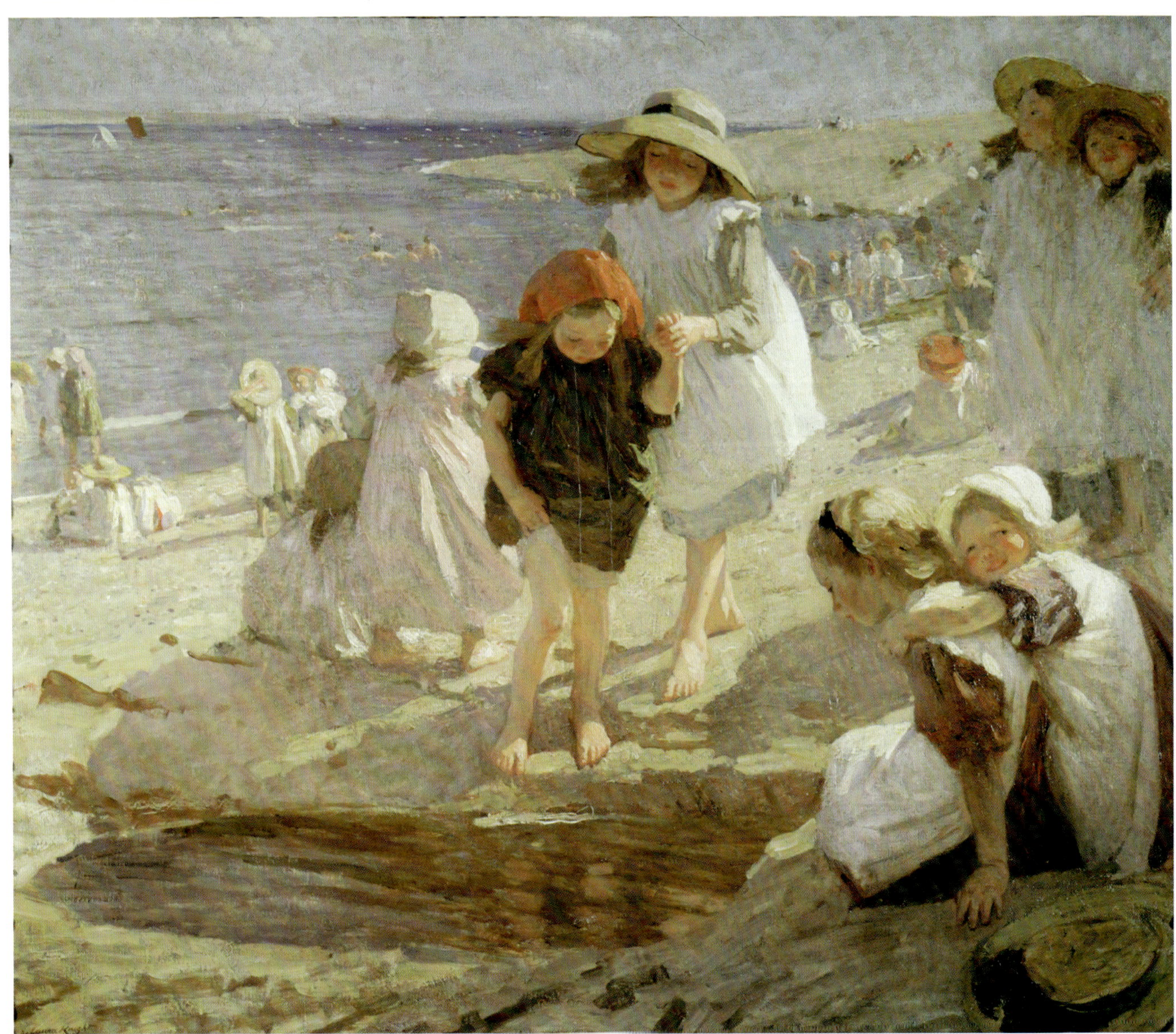

Dame Laura Knight (1877–1970)
The Beach, exhibited 1909
Oil on canvas, 127.6 x 153.2 cm
Purchased 1919
© Reproduced with permission of The Estate of Dame Laura Knight DBE RA. 2014. All Rights Reserved

Laura Knight is a very important figure in the history of art, most notably because in 1936 she became the first female member of the Royal Academy since the eighteenth century. Popular with fellow artists and the public alike during her lifetime, she remains one of Britain's favourite artists.

The Beach is a key picture produced by Knight during her time at Newlyn. Painted from sketches made on the beach, it captures the bright light and breeziness of the Cornish coast in summer. In a marked departure from her earlier muted, sombre colours, here she uses a much lighter palette to create a painting full of sunshine. Children often feature in her paintings and here they are scattered in small groups, peering into rock pools or playing in the waves. The low viewpoint and the way the children are arranged in the foreground make the viewer feel part of the scene, as the girl sitting on the right turns, smiling, to acknowledge their approach.

Sir Stanley Spencer (1891–1959)
The Lovers or _The Dustman_, 1934
Oil on canvas, 115 x 123.5 cm
Purchased 1948
© Tyne & Wear Archives & Museums/Bridgeman Images

Stanley Spencer was a devout Christian and believed God resided in all things. The miraculous, he thought, could be found in the everyday, and in his paintings ordinary people, events and objects are used to illustrate stories from the New Testament of the Bible and themes of Christian love. Rooted in the commonplace, his home village of Cookham in Berkshire became the setting for scenes from the life of Christ and other Biblical narratives.

The Lovers, also called *The Dustman*, is typical of Spencer's approach. His characteristic style has created an interlocking pattern of people and things as the dustman in the centre of the picture is being joyfully reunited with his wife after the Last Judgement, at the end of the world. He has leapt up into her arms and tenderly caresses her head as she turns to look at him. More labourers are coming down the path on the right, waiting to be reunited with their wives standing by the fence on the left.

Representing Spencer's joyful and optimistic view of life after death, *The Lovers* also illustrates the importance he placed on the small incidental items of domestic life, as he shows the 'resurrection' of thrown-away cabbage leaves, an empty jam pot and a broken teapot. Pulled from the dustbins by the children in the foreground and offered to the Dustman and his wife, Spencer felt that they were 'reminders of homelife and peace, and are worthy of being adored as the dustman is' (Stanley Spencer notebook, *c.*1936, Tate Archives, 733.3.74).

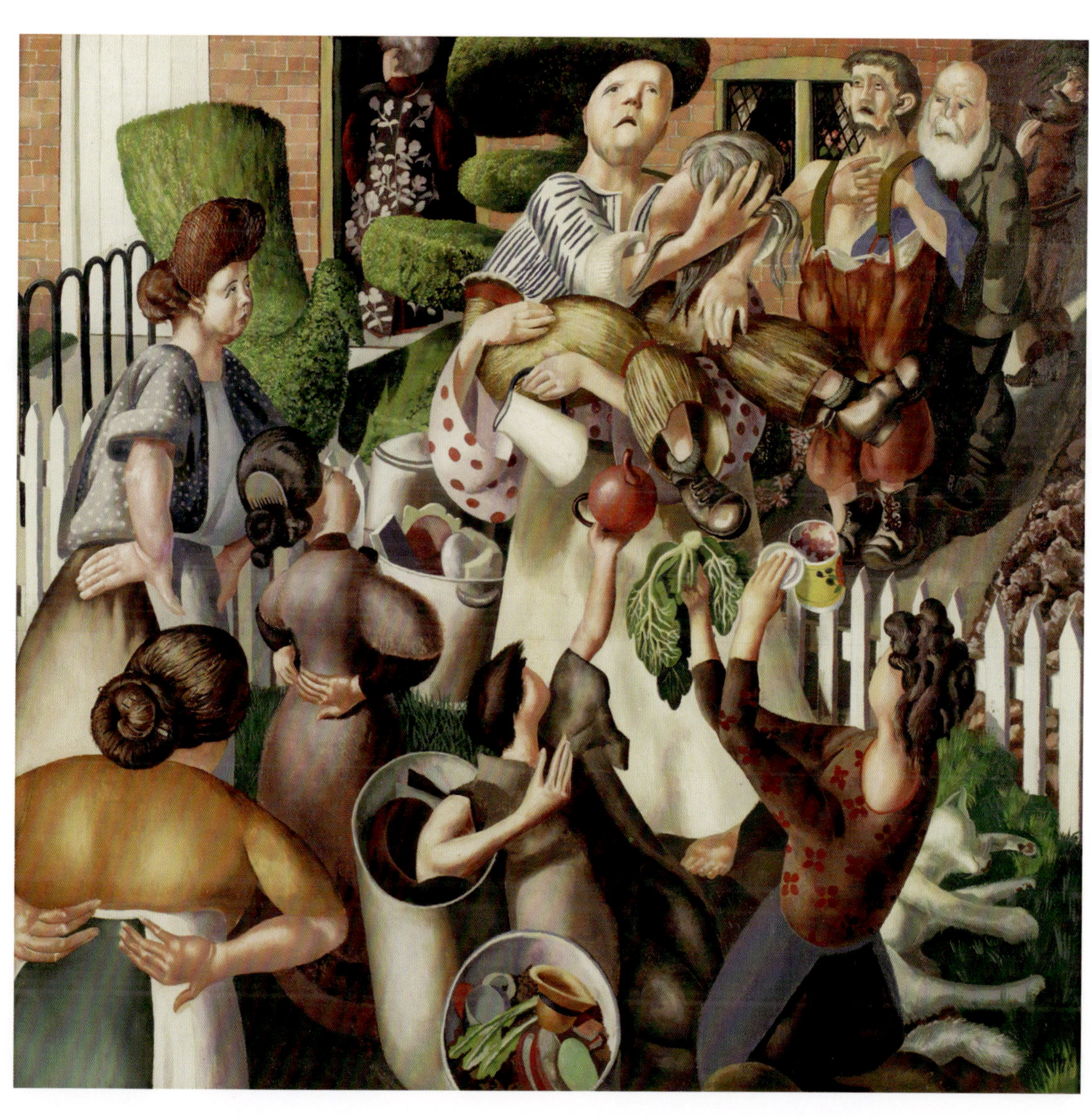

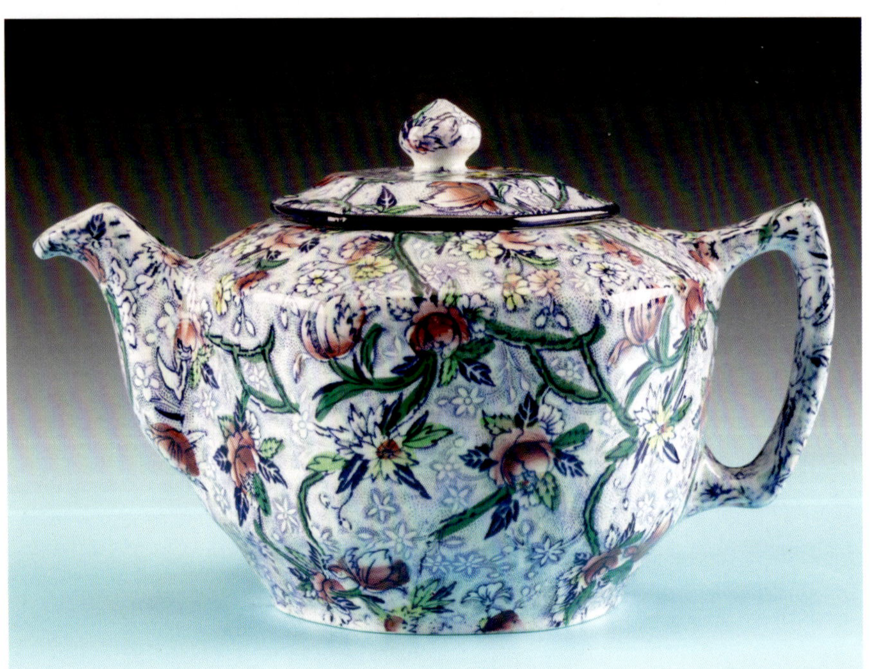

C.T. Maling & Sons (1762–1963)
Ringtons 'Chintz' Jug, 1930–40
Glazed earthenware with transfer-printed
and hand-painted decoration, 16 x 25 x 17 cm
Purchased 1975

The Maling pottery is closely associated with
another local firm, Ringtons tea merchants.
Between 1928 and 1962 Maling supplied
Ringtons with pottery, which the firm would
sell to its customers via their door-to-door
delivery vans, particularly during the
Christmas season. Maling produced a wide
range of tea caddies, teapots, vases, jugs and
souvenir wares in many different designs.
'Chintz' was one of the most popular, and
was used on a range of matching jugs and
teapots. However, the Maling paintresses
disliked it, as the design was 'fussy' and
difficult to paint.

Maling Pottery

For around 200 years Maling was among the most important
potteries of the North East. The first Maling Pottery was
opened in 1762 by William Maling at North Hylton, near
Sunderland. In 1817 the pottery moved to a new site on
Tyneside, at the Ouseburn Bridge, east of Newcastle. This was
a very successful move and throughout the nineteenth century
the firm continued to grow. It took over the existing Old
Ouseburn Pottery, and opened new, larger sites with the
Ford A (1859) and Ford B (1878) Potteries. Both Ford Potteries
were built by Christopher Thompson Maling, William's great-
grandson, who took over the firm on his father's death in 1863.
During his ownership the firm was at its most successful.
He introduced mechanisation and mass-production. In 1879,
Ford B was the largest pottery site in Great Britain, with ten
kilns and over a thousand employees. It was said to produce
more pots in a week than the old Ouseburn Bridge pottery
made in a year. Maling's was the largest, best-known and
longest-lived pottery firm on Tyneside. However, by the 1920s
trade was being damaged by competition from abroad, the
effects of the General Strike and the general trade depression.
The firm seemed to be recovering by the late 1930s, but
suffered another setback with the outbreak of the Second
World War. It struggled on, but never regained its former glory,
and eventually closed in June 1963, after over two centuries
of production.

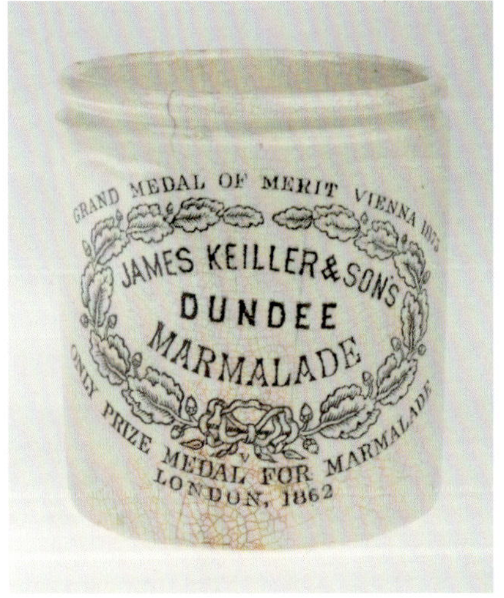

C.T. Maling & Sons
James Keiller & Sons Dundee Marmalade Pot, 1929
Glazed stoneware with transfer-printed label, 9.6 x 8.5 cm
Given by Mr S. Cottle, 1982

Although the Maling pottery is best known for its decorative wares,
it was founded on the production of plain, commercial pottery, such
as jam jars and preserve pots. This type of work continued to provide
a large part of the factory's income throughout its life. Keiller's of
Dundee, makers of jams and marmalades, was one of the factory's
main customers from the mid-1800s to the 1930s. The jars Maling
produced for Keiller's ranged from a massive 2-pound jar to a
miniature version, one of which was used to furnish the kitchen in
Queen Mary's famous dolls' house.

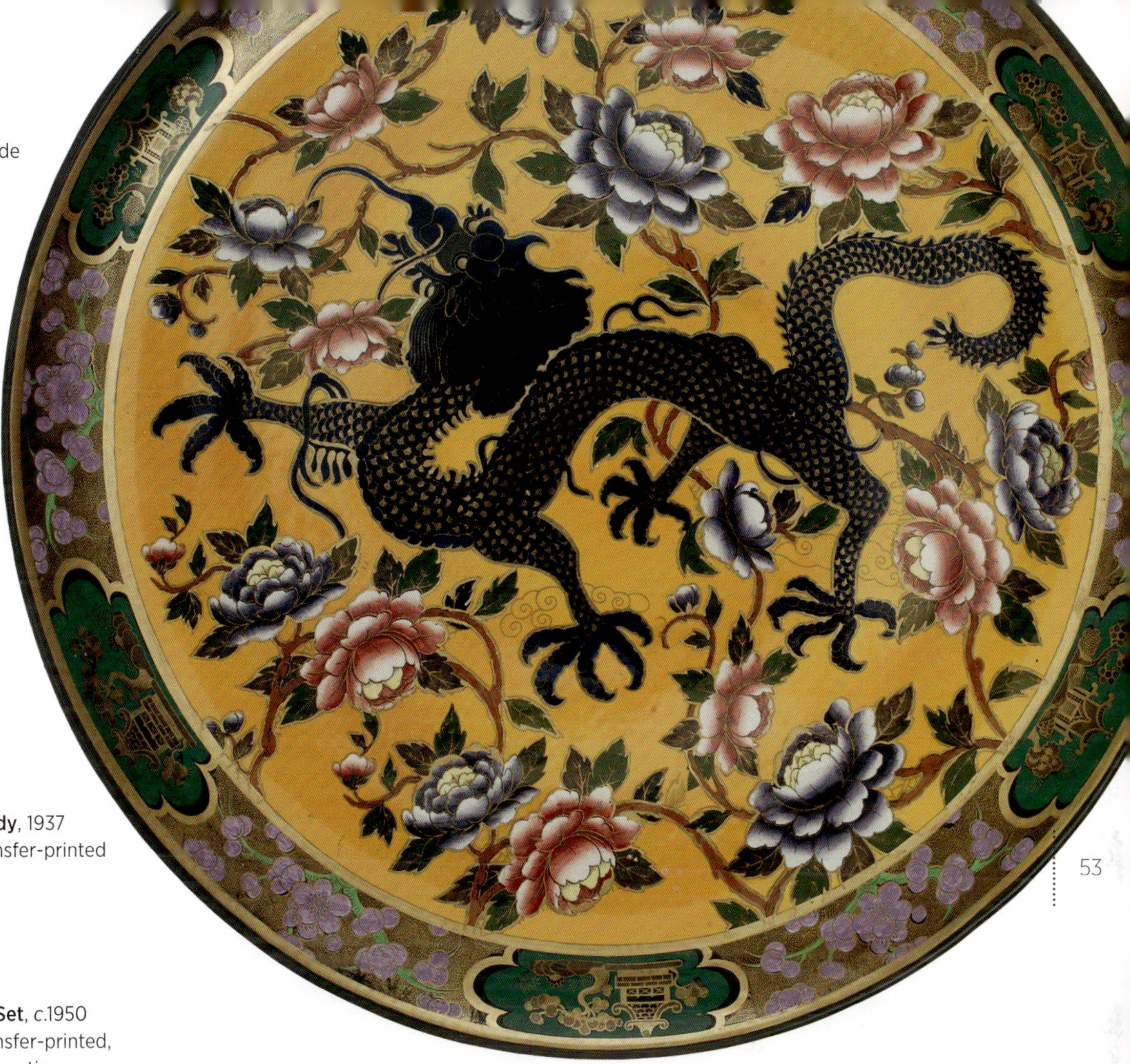

C.T. Maling & Sons
'Oriental' Dragon Plaque, made
1888, decorated *c.*1929
Earthenware with transfer-
printed, hand-painted and
gilded decoration,
6.5 x 54.5 cm
Purchased with grant aid
from the Victoria and Albert
Museum Purchase Grant
Fund, 1989

Below left:
C.T. Maling & Sons
Ringtons George VI Tea Caddy, 1937
Glazed earthenware with transfer-printed
decoration, 19 x 16 x 12 cm
Purchased 1975

Below right:
C.T. Maling & Sons
'Springtime' Dressing Table Set, *c.*1950
Glazed earthenware with transfer-printed,
hand-painted and gilded decoration,
tray 2 x 29.5 x 16 cm, candlestick 6.5 x 10 cm,
bowl 6.5 x 12 cm
Purchased 1975

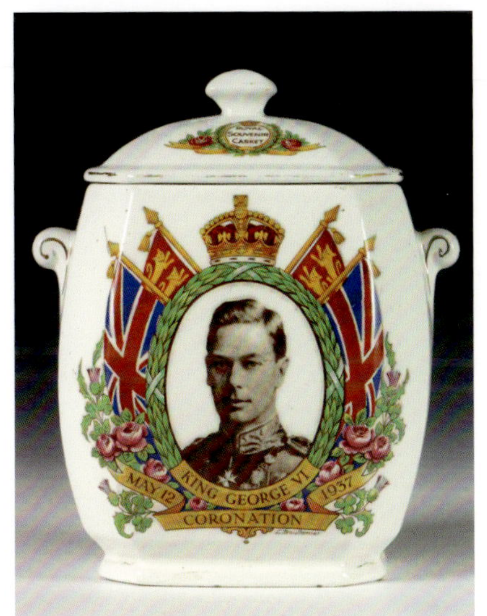

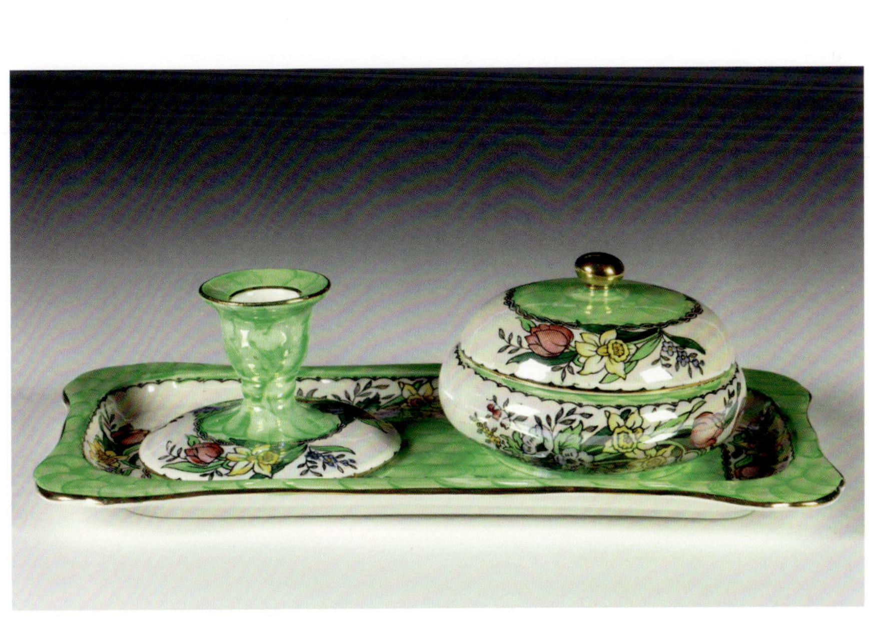

Ben Nicholson (1894–1982)
1933 (design), 1933
Oil and pencil on wood, 25.4 x 51.6 cm
Given by the Contemporary Art Society, 1946
© Angela Verren Taunt 2014. All Rights Reserved,
DACS

Ben Nicholson was a key figure in the development
of British abstract art during the 1930s and central
to the group of Modernist artists at St Ives.
Together with that of sculptor Henry Moore, his
work is often described as the epitome of British
Modernism. Nicholson's earliest pieces were still
lifes, influenced by those of his father, the painter Sir
William Nicholson. He travelled throughout Europe,
especially visiting France, Italy and Switzerland,
and after seeing the work of Pablo Picasso and
other artists in France, in the 1920s began painting
figurative and abstract works inspired by Post-
Impressionism and Cubism. From 1924 to 1936,
together with his first wife the painter Winifred
Nicholson, he was a leading member of and
exhibitor with the pioneering Seven & Five Society.
Then, in 1933, he joined Unit One, a group of British
Modernist artists founded by Paul Nash and including Henry Moore, Barbara Hepworth and Edward
Burra. That same year Nicholson produced his first
geometric and abstract reliefs, as well as making
1933 (design).

In this piece the two parts of the composition
show Nicholson's interest in the relationship between
representational and abstract art. The head on the
left seems almost like a simplified design on a
Roman coin. He was also fascinated by the 'musical'
relationship between form, tone and colour, and has
scraped some of the surface of the paint to produce
tonal variations. These contrast with areas of bright,
flat red paint and white colour, which give the
impression of jumping forward. Together, these
features create a shifting sense of space.

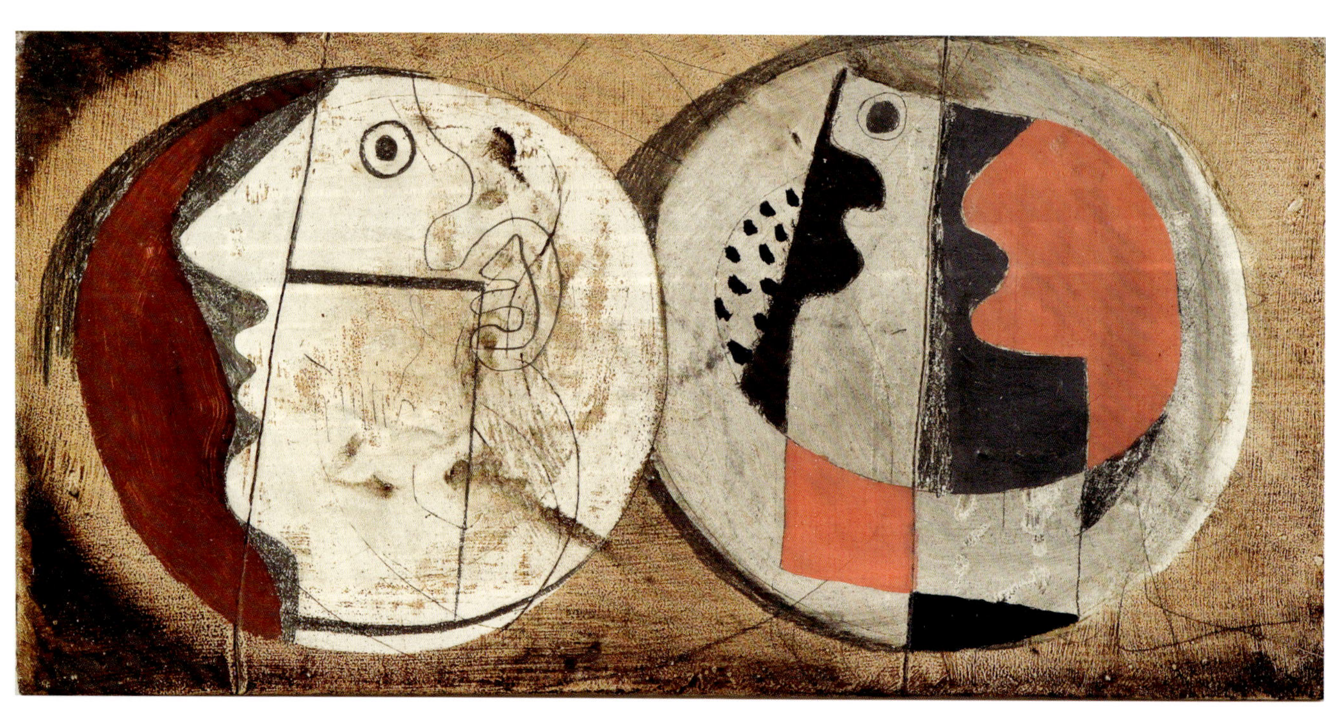

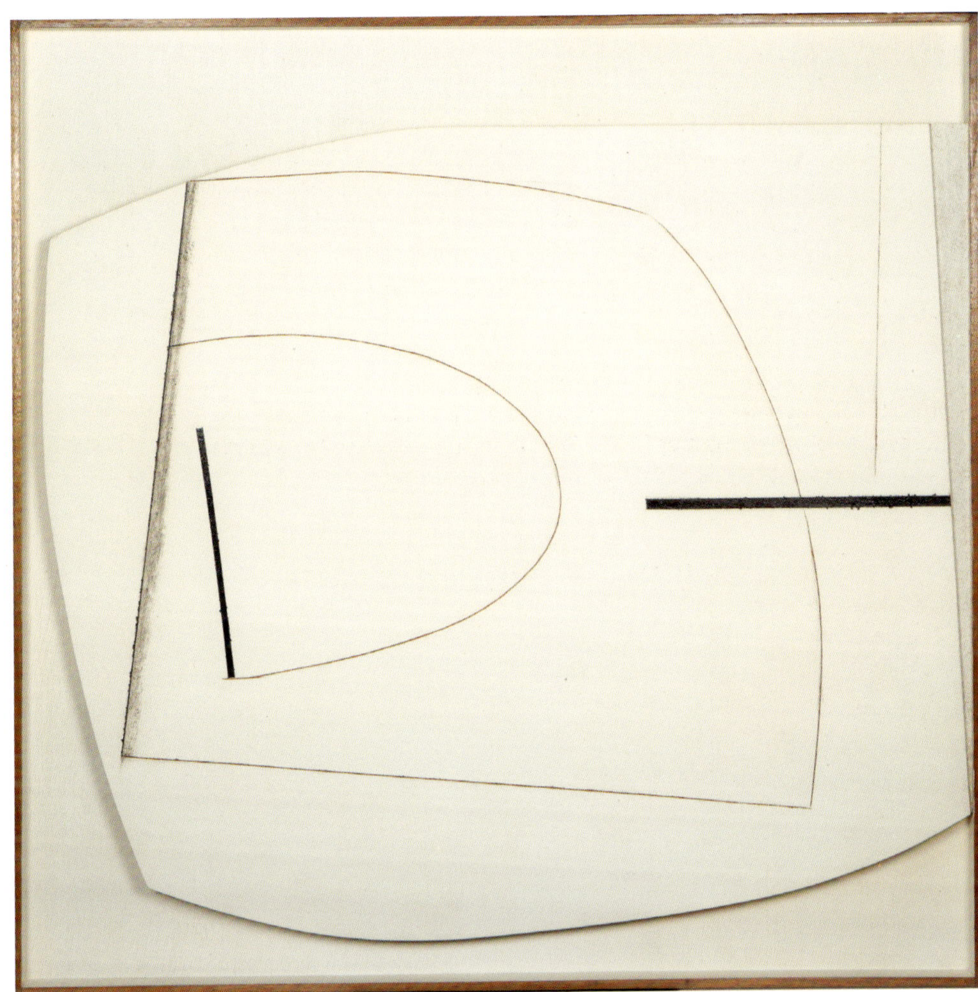

Victor Pasmore (1908–1998)
Linear Motif in Black and White, *c.*1959–60
Painted relief, oil on wood, 123 x 123 cm
Purchased with grant aid from the Victoria and Albert Museum Purchase Grant Fund, The Art Fund and Friends of the Laing Art Gallery, 2009
© Estate of Victor Pasmore. All Rights Reserved, DACS 2014

The artist and architect Victor Pasmore was a pioneer in the development of British Abstract Expressionism during the 1940s and 1950s. His early work was figurative, with conventional landscape and still-life scenes, but he became interested in abstraction during the 1930s. From 1943 to 1949, he taught at Camberwell School of Art, where he promoted abstract art and reform of the fine art education system. In 1952 he was appointed Head of the Department of Painting at King's College (now Newcastle University) and developed a new arts and design course based on the 'basic course' of the Bauhaus, an art school in Germany renowned for its approach to design. Pasmore's course went on to become a model for higher arts education across the UK.

After 1947, and under the influence of artists such as Ben Nicholson, Pasmore developed a purely abstract style, becoming a leading figure in the post-war revival of interest in British Constructivism. His work often involved collage and the construction of reliefs, using innovative materials, and was frequently on a grand, architectural scale. *Linear Motif in Black and White* is typical of his reliefs during the late 1950s and early 1960s, with layers of smooth and textured wood creating three-dimensional space and actual shadows. He then added scored and painted lines to the surface in varying intensities. Shortly after completing it, Pasmore represented Britain at the Venice Biennale of Art in 1960, a measure of the esteem in which his work was held.

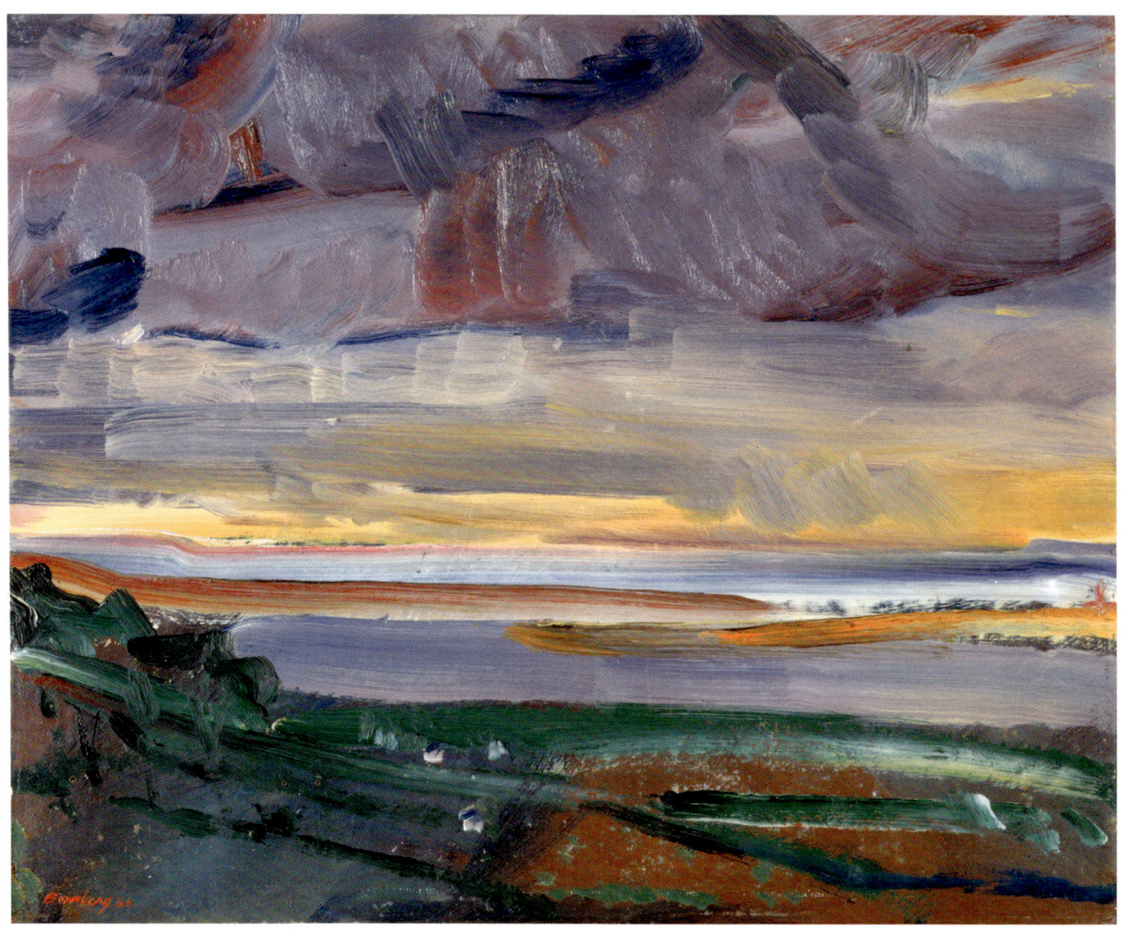

David Bomberg (1890–1957)
Sunset, The Bay, North Devon, 1946
Oil on canvas, 61.2 x 76.3 cm
Purchased 1952
© The Estate of David Bomberg.
All Rights Reserved, DACS 2014

David Bomberg is considered one of the most audacious painters of his generation. His early work was heavily influenced by Cubism and Futurism: complex, geometric compositions featuring angular figures and forms bursting with energy. His methods were so radical that he was expelled from the Slade School of Art in 1913, as he was considered too far removed from the conventional approach of the time. However, after serving as a soldier in the trenches during the First World War, he became disillusioned with the 'machine age' and his work became increasingly dominated by portraits and landscapes, and themes drawn from nature.
He also began to work in a much more Expressionist style, and travelled widely throughout Europe and the Middle East.

Bomberg created this scene during a summer painting trip to the village of Instow in Devon. It shows Bideford Bay viewed from the top of the cliffs, where he pitched his tent. The stormy sky and gathering twilight are represented by reddish purples and blues set against the gold streak of sunset on the horizon. These rich colours express the powerful emotions that he felt for the landscape, while broad, creamy brushstrokes add to the sensuousness of the colour. Bomberg considered this to be one of his best Expressionist landscapes; at the time the Laing Art Gallery purchased it, he wrote a letter to the Gallery's curator describing it as 'a work of my highest achievement' (letter from David Bomberg to C. Bernard Stephenson, 5 April 1952).

Gillian Ayres (born 1930)
Papua, 1988
Oil on canvas, 274.3 x 274.4 cm
Purchased with grant aid from the
Victoria and Albert Museum Purchase
Grant Fund, 1990
Courtesy Gillian Ayres

Gillian Ayres is one of Britain's most
important abstract artists. Her early work
developed in response to the combined
influences of American Abstract
Expressionism and European art from
Titian to Claude Monet and Henri
Matisse. Her painting then and since has
been characterised by enormous vitality
and emotional intensity, large scale,
vibrant use of colour, and the tactility
of the paint, which she applies in many
layers, using her hands as well as brushes.
Her paintings have always been non-
objective and her early works deliberately
avoided single-focus compositions or
any suggestion that the paintings were
illustrations.

Papua bursts with the energy created
by rich texture, vigorous marks and
powerful colour. Ayres's paintings from
the 1980s demonstrate a change in her
style, the shapes referring more explicitly
to the world of natural forms, more
strongly gestural, and in general more
focused. She has always been known as
a colourist, but these paintings are, if
anything, even more exuberantly
colourful than before. When *Papua* was
first shown in London, Ayres chose a
poem called 'Two Colours' by French
writer Yves Bonnefoy to accompany it
in the catalogue:

Further than the star
In the reflection
Two hands delve, having nothing to hold with
but their own trust
Two hands, broken, search
For better than gold
And that life be born
Of nothing but a dream

(Yves Bonnefoy, quoted in *Gillian Ayres*,
Arnolfini/Knoedler Kasmin Ltd, May 1989, p.4)

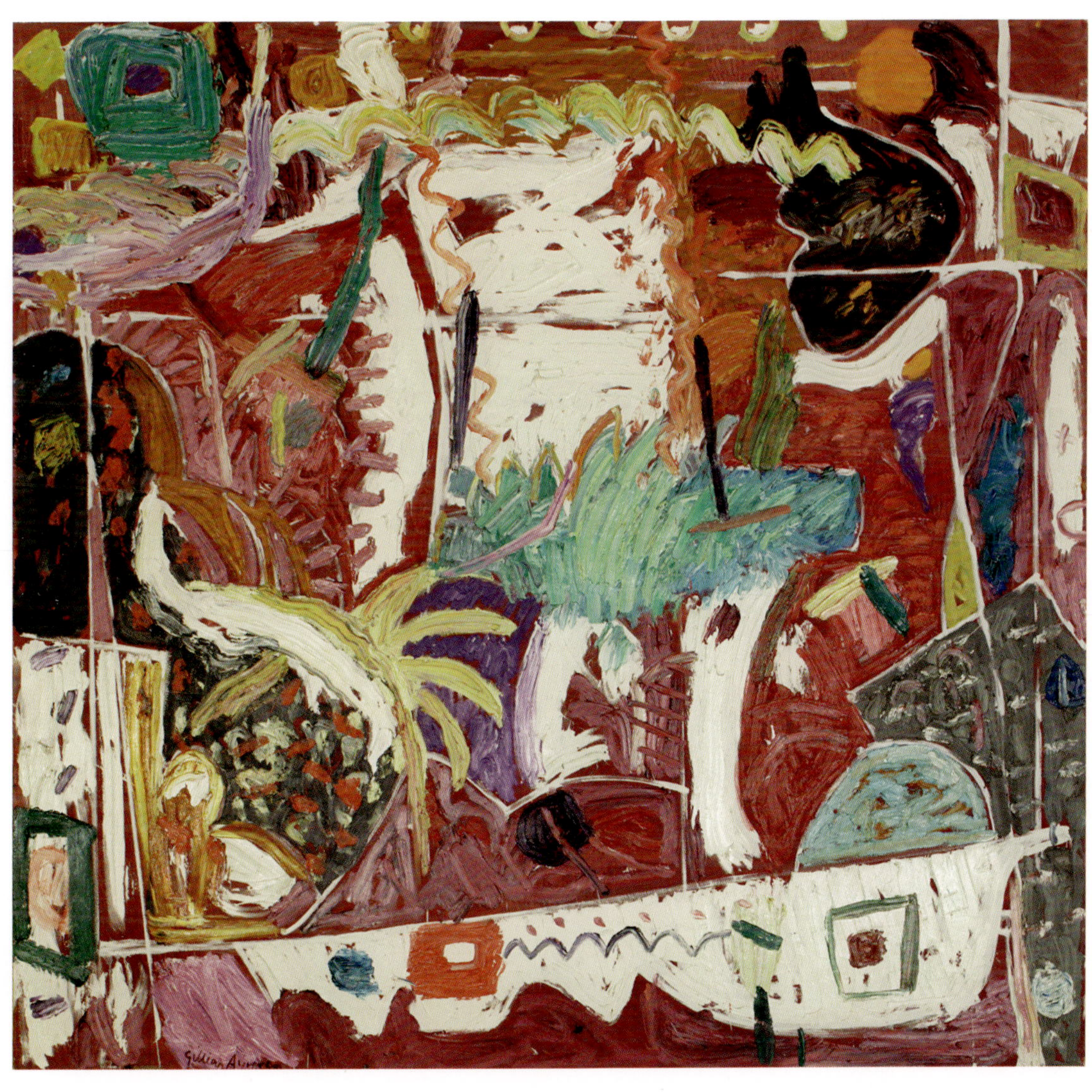

Henry Moore (1898–1986)
Seated Woman: Thin Neck, 1961
Displayed within the *Paul Noble Marble Hall*
Bronze, 161.7 x 71.2 x 106.7 cm
Purchased with grant aid from the Victoria and Albert Museum
Purchase Grant Fund, 1964
Reproduced by permission of The Henry Moore Foundation

Henry Moore is considered one of the most important British sculptors of the twentieth century. Internationally renowned, he is best known for his semi-abstract, monumental sculptures in stone or bronze, which can be found in collections around the world. His sculptures are usually abstractions of the human figure, often pierced or containing hollow spaces, and influenced by shapes derived from the natural world – bones, shells, stones or landscape forms.

The combination of figurative and abstract features in *Seated Woman: Thin Neck* is characteristic of Moore's work. The thin neck of the woman was inspired by the breast-bone of a bird, which has great strength despite its lightness, while the massive thighs suggest the outlines of a rocky landscape. It also represents a transition in Moore's style from the rounded, reclining figures of the 1940s and 1950s, with their soft and organic shapes, to the more angular, fragmented and abstract constructions of the late 1960s. Moore often made small maquettes (trial models) of his sculptures from pieces of clay, later scaling them up for casting in bronze, and the smooth, curved back of this sculpture suggests the model was cradled in the palm of the sculptor's hand as he worked on it.

The sculpture is the sixth in a series of eight. Today, six of the others are in museums and galleries in the USA and the remaining one is owned by Tate, London.

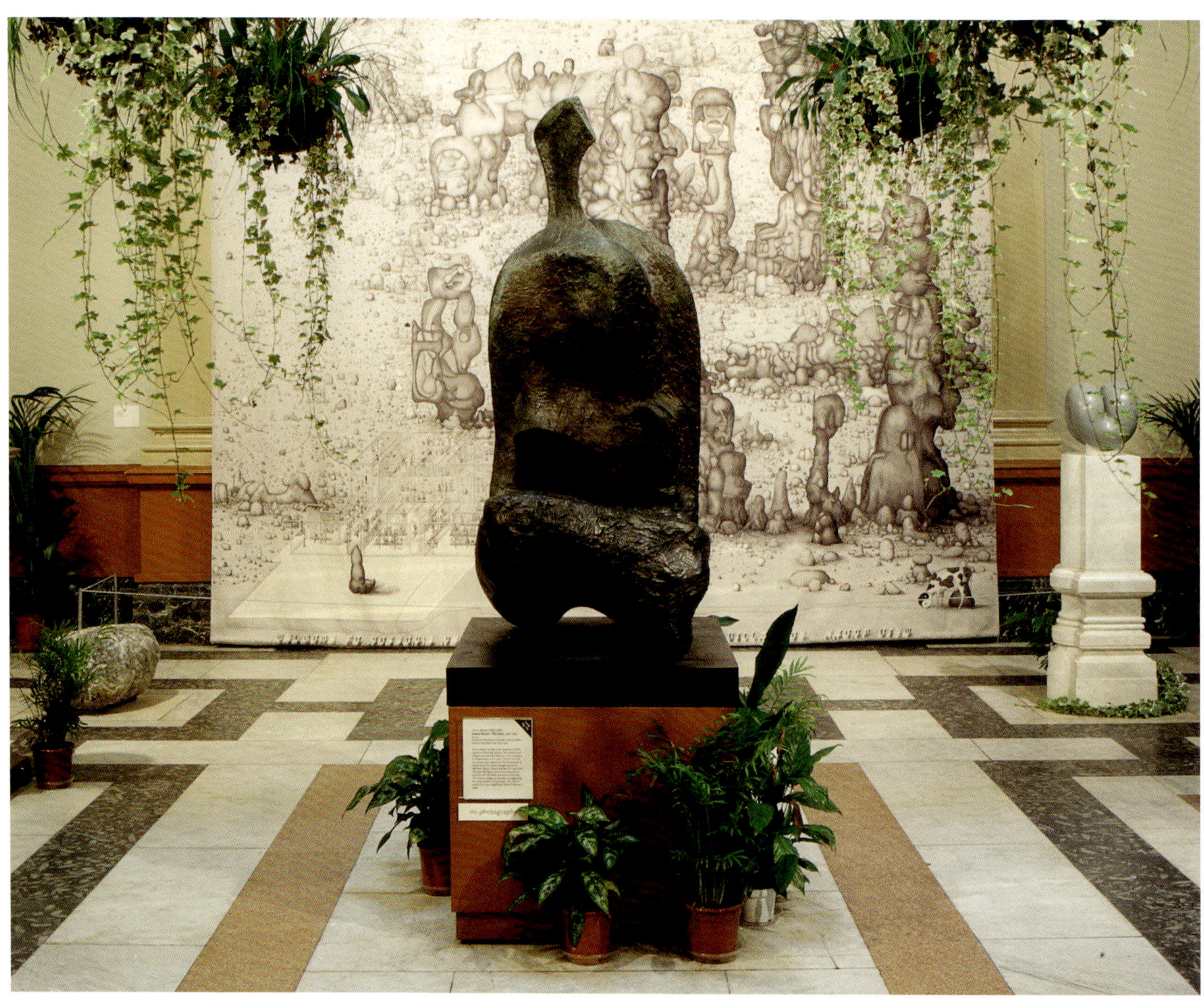

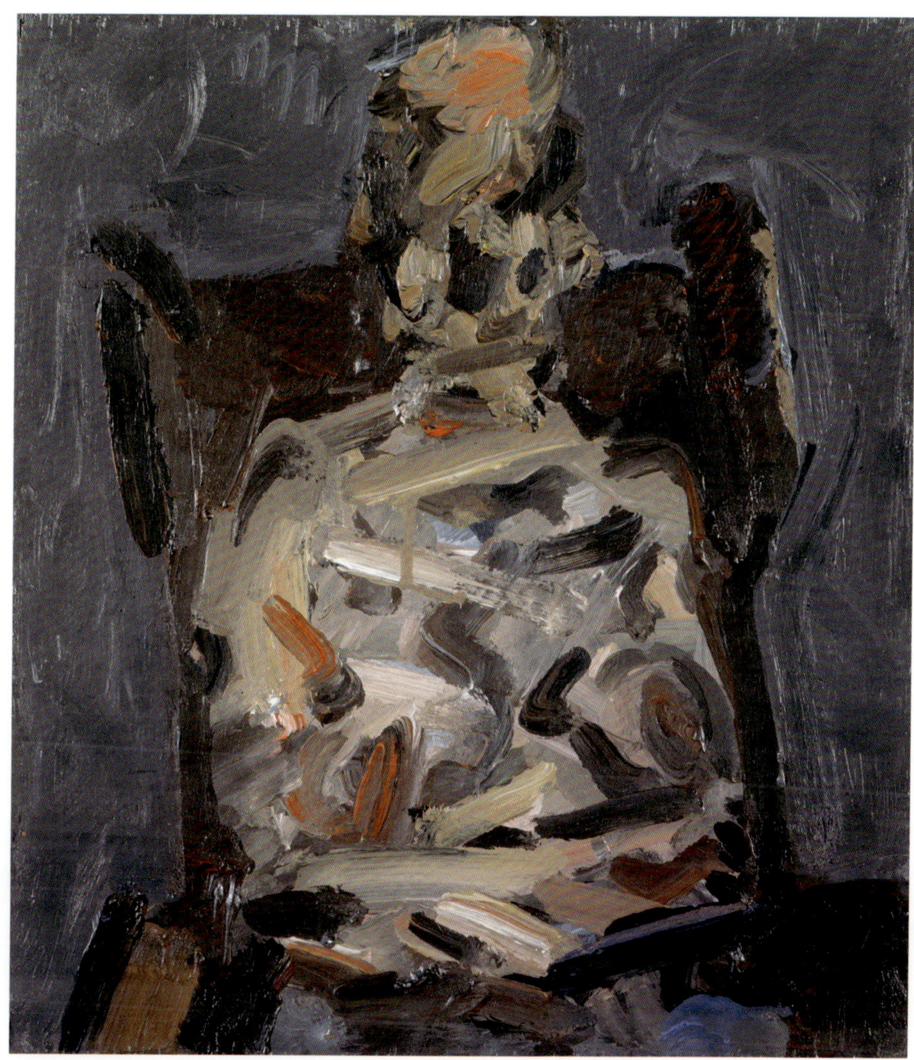

Frank Auerbach (born 1931)
Julia, 1987
Acrylic on wood, 45.8 x 40.6 cm
Purchased with grant aid from the Victoria and Albert Museum
Purchase Grant Fund, The Art Fund and Friends of the Laing
Art Gallery, 1987
© Frank Auerbach, courtesy Marlborough Fine Art

Frank Auerbach is an internationally renowned artist, part of
the group of leading figurative painters known as the School of
London, which also included Lucien Freud. Born in Berlin to a
German-Jewish family, he was sent to Britain at the age of
eight, just before the outbreak of the Second World War, and
later studied in London, particularly under the tuition of David
Bomberg. Auerbach's pictures seem challengingly different
from what one might expect from portrait likenesses. However,
they are rooted in a long tradition of figure painting, and the
work of Walter R. Sickert, Willem de Kooning, and Rembrandt
van Rijn has been particularly influential.

Julia is one of a series of warm and intimate portraits of
Auerbach's wife, which he painted after they re-established
contact following a long separation. A personal relationship
with the sitter is critical to Auerbach, whose pictures are
attempts, reworked over many sessions, to distil the presence
of the sitter. He aims to present his subject in very direct terms,
to achieve a sense of raw reality and of physical mass brought
alive by an inner spirit. *Julia* is painted with the technique
Auerbach adopted in the second half of his career. Instead of
building layer upon layer of paint, he scraped off the previous
day's work at the beginning of each session. This enabled him
to maintain an intensity of concentration over a long period,
while developing a freer and more spontaneous style.

Eduardo Paolozzi (1924–2005)
Sack-O-Sauce (from the series 'Bunk!'),
1972
Screenprint, 36.1 x 27.7 cm
Purchased 1979

Scottish artist Eduardo Paolozzi was a
sculptor, collagist, printmaker and film-
maker. He attended Edinburgh College
of Art in 1943 then, after a brief military
service, studied at St Martin's School
of Art in London and the Slade School
of Fine Art, where he specialised in
sculpture. From 1947 to 1949 he worked
in Paris, meeting artists including
Alberto Giacometti, Constantin Brâncuşi
and Georges Braque, and became
acquainted with Surrealist art.

In 1952 Paolozzi gave a lecture
entitled 'Bunk' at the Institute of
Contemporary Art in London as part of
the Independent Group. 'Bunk' is short
for 'bunkum' and is American slang for
rubbish or nonsense. It also refers to the
American car manufacturer Henry
Ford's famous statement that 'history is
more or less bunk'. Paolozzi presented a
selection of images taken from science
fiction and other popular magazines
given to him by American ex-
servicemen. They showed Paolozzi's
fascination with popular culture and
technology, as well as with the glamour
of American consumerism, mixing
washing machines and war machines,
Coca-Cola bottles and cartoons,
parodying post-war consumer society.
The idea was revolutionary at the time
and provoked heated debate. 'Bunk' is
now seen as the earliest forerunner of
Pop Art, and as a result of the lectures
Paolozzi created the 'Bunk!' print series
in 1972.

The prints in 'Bunk!' were based on
elaborate collages: most of the images
are hand torn, creased and glued to
paper, then reproduced using screen-
printing and lithographic printing
techniques. Employing Disney
characters and images of aeroplanes
and machines, clips of magazine text and
abstract patterns, Paolozzi referred to his
collages as 'ready-made metaphors for
the dreams of the masses' (E. Paolozzi,
'About the prints: the artist talking at an
interview', interview with C. Hogben and
E. Bailey, in F. Whitford et al., *Bunk:
A Box-file of Images in Print*, exh. cat.
(London: Victoria and Albert Museum,
1973), unpaginated).

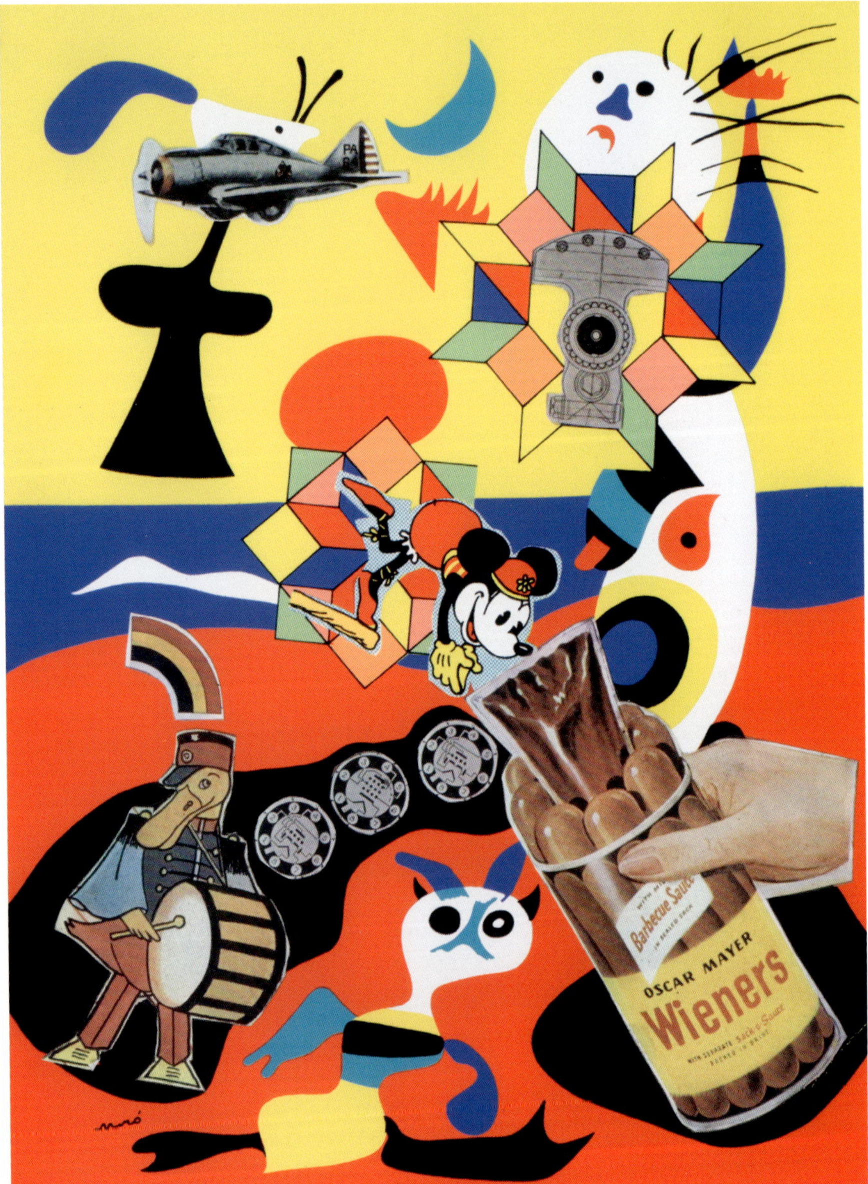

Dame Elizabeth Blackadder (born 1931)
*Still Life with Japanese Swordguards
and Fans*, 1990
Fibre, gold leaf and watercolour on
paper, 76 x 50.5 cm
Purchased with grant aid from the
Victoria and Albert Museum Purchase
Grant Fund, 1992
© the artist

Elizabeth Blackadder is an important
figure in the field of watercolour
painting. The first woman to be a
member of both the Royal Academy
in London and the Royal Scottish
Academy, in 1982 she was awarded an
OBE for her contribution to art. In 2001
she was appointed 'Her Majesty's Painter
and Limner in Scotland' and in 2003 she
was made a Dame. Blackadder has also
been awarded honorary doctorates by
four universities. She works in a range
of media and techniques, including oil
paint, watercolour, drawing and print-
making. Blackadder is perhaps best
known for her still-life compositions,
often featuring cats and flowers. Her
work is extremely detailed, with careful
consideration of the use of space within
the composition.

Following visits to Japan in 1985 and
1986, Blackadder became fascinated
with the techniques and subjects of
Eastern art. Avoiding the technological
modernity of Tokyo, she was instead
drawn to the Zen gardens of Kyoto, and
her work from this time often expresses
the principles of Zen, especially the
importance it places on empty space.
She was also impressed by Japanese
artists' use of textured paper and
explored its possibilities in works such as
*Still Life with Japanese Swordguards and
Fans.* Here she combines the rough,
fibrous paper with gold leaf along the
bottom edge of the composition, which
together with dense, vibrant colours
contributes additional richness to the
image. The inspiration of Japanese art is
present in the swordguards, swordcase
and fans, and the simple rounded
mountains in blue and green.

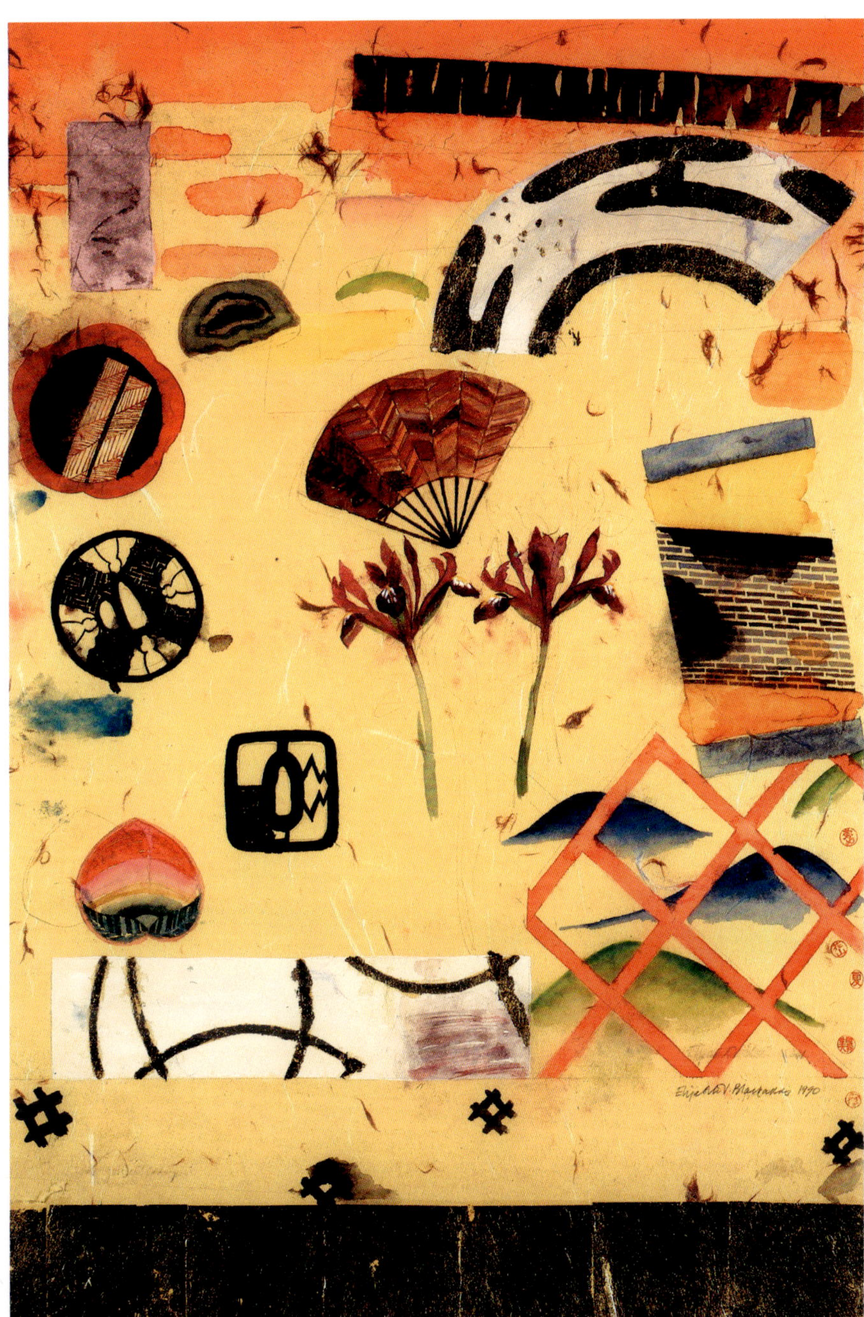

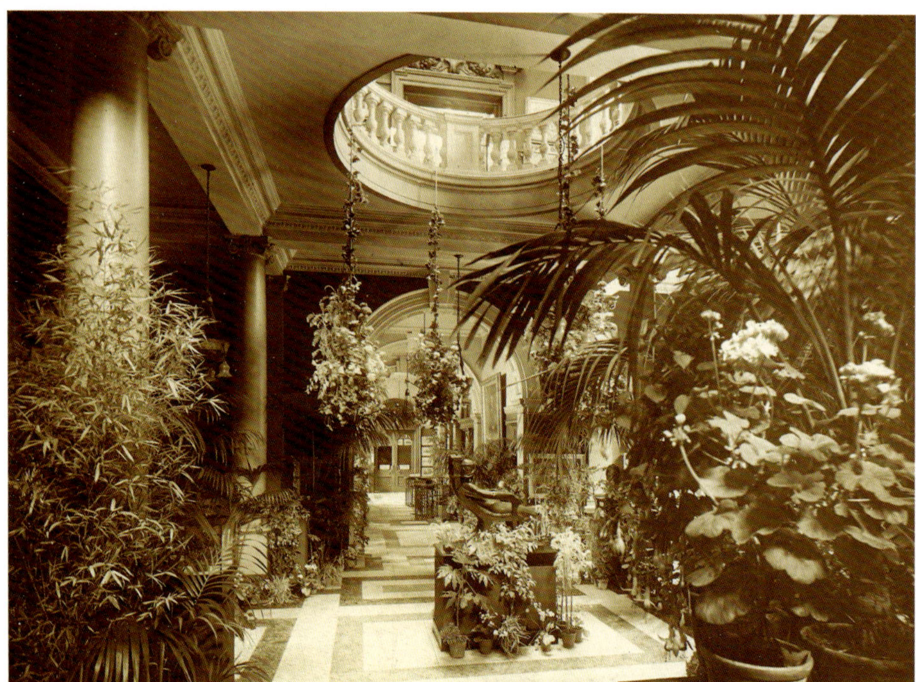

The Marble Hall in the Laing Art Gallery,
early twentieth century

Below:
Paul Noble
seven, 2006–7
Glazed ceramic, walnut base,
59.7 x 65.1 x 39.1 cm
Given by the artist, 2013
Photo by Mike Bruce. Courtesy
Gagosian Gallery
© Paul Noble

IN FOCUS

Paul Noble Marble Hall

Paul Noble (born 1963) was nominated for the Turner Prize in 2012 and has exhibited in New York as well as at Tate, London. He grew up in Whitley Bay on the North East coast and aspects of his work are strongly inspired by his experiences there. In 2010, he was commissioned to create *Paul Noble Marble Hall* (see inside back cover), a one-off installation and intervention, as part of an evolving programme of display and rethinking of the presentation of art in the Marble Hall at the Laing.

Paul Noble Marble Hall situates Noble's own art, centred on his huge tapestry *villa joe*, within the historical context of the Laing's architecture and collections. Using archive photographs dating from around the time of the opening of the Gallery in 1904, the artist re-created the appearance of the Hall when it was filled with plants. The plants also refer to Noble's interest in exploring the boundary between the natural world and cultural constructs. This theme is echoed in the images on his 'artist designed' wallpaper, featuring antique plinths interspersed with vegetation.

Paul Noble's tapestry has been purchased for the Gallery with the aid of substantial grants. The artist has made a gift of a ceramic sculpture, *seven*, which was part of a large group incorporated in the original installation. The piece is covered with thick shiny glaze inspired by those used in traditional Japanese ceramics. It is presented on a carved wooden stand

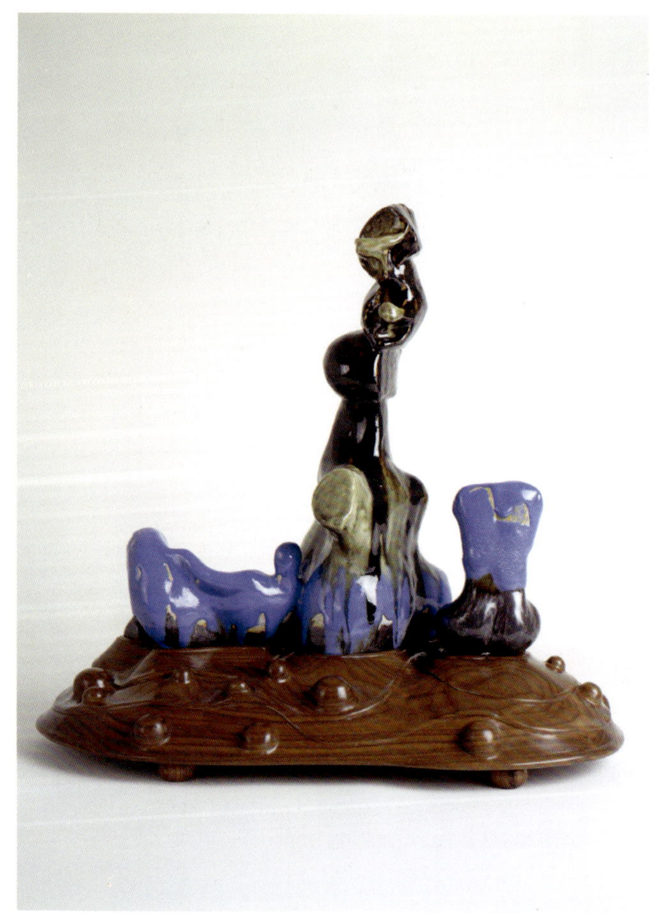

Paul Noble
villa joe, 2010
Wool tapestry,
456 x 440 cm
Purchased with
grant aid from the
Victoria and Albert
Museum Purchase
Grant Fund, The Art
Fund and Friends
of the Laing Art
Gallery, 2013
© the artist

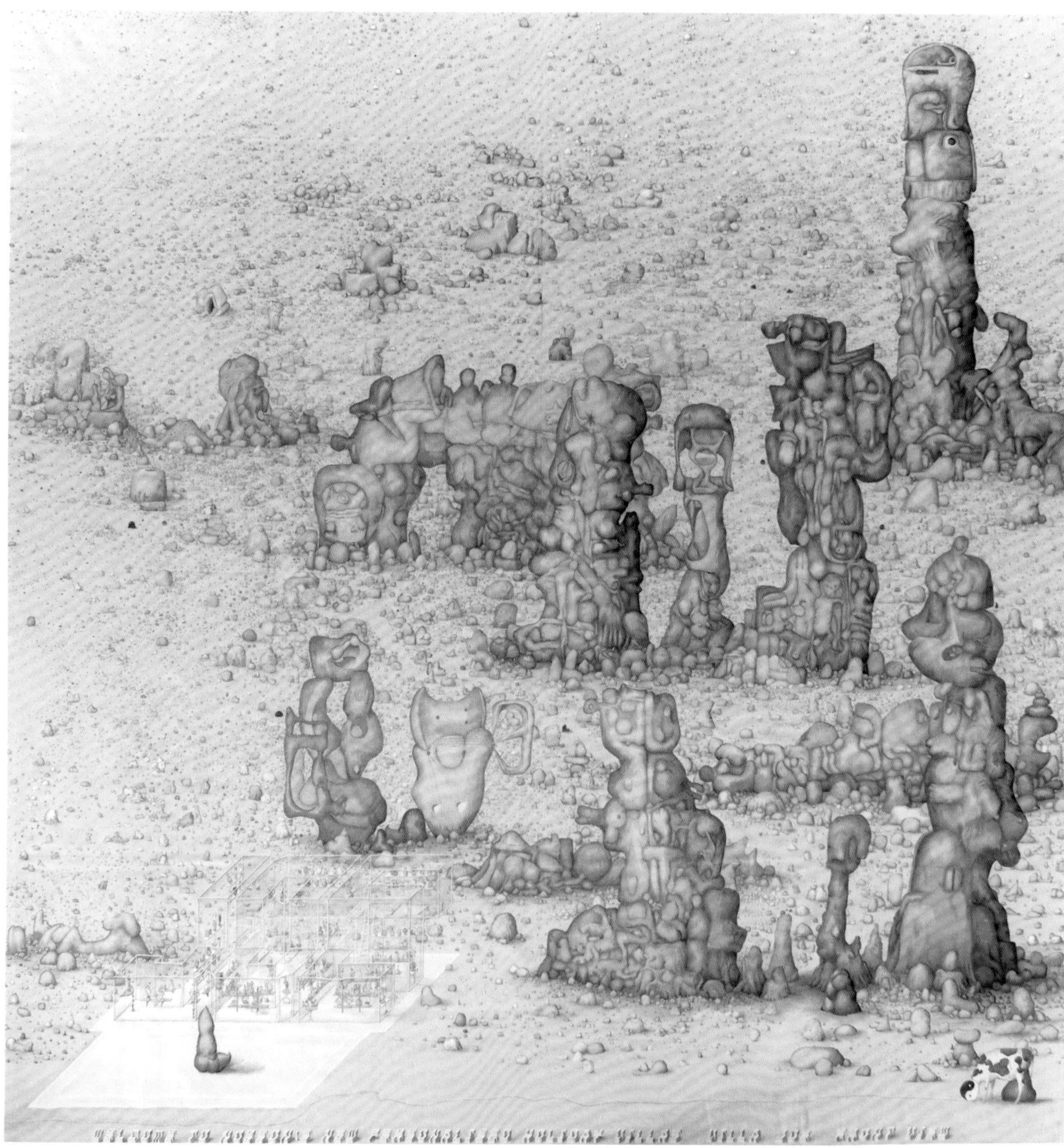

in the style of Chinese 'scholars' stones' – rocks selected for their shape and surface that are placed on pedestals.

The tapestry and ceramic link directly to the Laing Art Gallery's collection, and central to the installation is Henry Moore's large bronze sculpture *Seated Woman: Thin Neck* (see page 58). Noble has made an in-depth study of Moore, who famously liked to go beachcombing in search of flints and pebbles eroded into inspiring shapes. Noble's ceramics are diminutive versions of the organic sculptures made by Moore in response to his beachcombing collection, reducing the monumentality of Moore's sculptures to the scale and status of ornaments.

The ceramic piece realises in three-dimensional form the precious collection of objects housed in 'villa joe', which features in Noble's tapestry of the same title. The building is named after Joseph Holtzman, Editor-in-Chief and Art Director of the cult décor magazine *Nest*, who is known for his meticulously hyper-decorated Manhattan apartment, in which the juxtaposition of every object is fine-tuned. Through the glass walls of Holtzman's 'museum', as shown in the bottom left-hand side of the tapestry, one can see the exhibits neatly laid out. There is a jarring contrast between the modern display of objects within and the rough, monumental forms of the surrounding landscape.

Index